SPECTACULAR HOMES
of Greater Washington, D.C.

AN EXCLUSIVE SHOWCASE OF DESIGNERS IN WASHINGTON, D.C., NORTHERN VIRGINIA & MARYLAND

Published by

PANACHE
PANACHE PARTNERS, LLC

13747 Montfort Drive, Suite 100
Dallas, Texas 75240
972.661.9884
972.661.2743
www.panache.com

Publishers: Brian G. Carabet and John A. Shand
Executive Publisher: Phil Reavis
Associate Publisher: Kathryn Newell
Art Director: Michele Cunningham-Scott
Editor: Sarah Toler

Printed in Malaysia

Distributed by Gibbs Smith, Publisher
800.748.5439

PUBLISHER'S DATA

Spectacular Homes of Greater Washington, D.C.

Library of Congress Control Number: 2006935835

ISBN - 13: 978-1-933415-20-8
ISBN - 10: 1-933415-20-7

First Printing 2006

10 9 8 7 6 5 4 3 2 1

Previous Page: Barry Dixon, Inc.
See page 187 Photograph by Gordon Beall

This Page: Aidan Design
See page 167 Photograph by Fredde Lieberman and Robert Radifera

SPECTACULAR HOMES
of Greater Washington, D.C.

AN EXCLUSIVE SHOWCASE OF DESIGNERS IN WASHINGTON, D.C., NORTHERN VIRGINIA & MARYLAND

foreword

Washington, D.C. is a unique and special place to those of us lucky enough to call it home. The sweeping hunt country of Virginia is to our west and further still, the grandeur of the Blue Ridge Mountains. To our east is the picturesque Chesapeake Bay into which our rambling and powerful Potomac River flows past the monuments and cherry blossoms, past the old tobacco farms and cotton fields to the very place Pocahontas stood with her father, Powhatan, and watched John Smith come ashore.

Yet today, we celebrate a new technology industry, vibrant theatre and cultural institutions and are the home to seven universities. Our homes are as diverse as our cultures and our careers. Whether we come from the world of government, education, technology, real estate or business, our homes, like us, are special and unique. The Federal townhouses of Capitol Hill and Georgetown offer a unique set of challenges, while the luxurious and opulent new homes of McLean and Potomac offer their own. And some of our most charming homes can be found in the bungalows of Bethesda and Chevy Chase, now all redone by the world class designers found amongst these pages.

Washington is rich in tradition; part of that tradition is to entertain in the home. So our homes are known to be warm and uncluttered; sophisticated and yet down to earth. Clients want their homes both to be impressive and approachable. This can be a daunting task, and it requires not only talent but years of study and practice. This explains the worldwide attention and acclaim that many of our designers are now enjoying.

I have had the opportunity in my life to see many homes around the world designed by the most famous designers of their time; Nancy Lancaster, Billy Baldwin, Billy Haines, Dorothy Draper, Sister Parrish and others. The designers working in Washington, D.C. today are proudly paralleling their venerable forebearers. I have enjoyed the casual elegance of London and Paris and thought that we could never duplicate it ... this book proves I was wrong. Within these pages, you will find the subtleties and restraint that define good taste. Nowhere could that be more appropriate than in a place that Washington and Jefferson picked as the nation's home.

Deborah Gore Dean

Deborah Gore Dean

introduction

As you turn the pages of *Spectacular Homes of Greater Washington, D.C.*, you will see and feel the vibrancy of the capital's history juxtaposed with the creativity of contemporary designers. The diversity of the landscape and the people within this region offer a canvas for talented decorators and interior designers to unleash their artistry and bring to life each client's vision of home.

The beautiful homes that grace these pages range from wonderful old rowhouses in Georgetown to stately mansions on the Potomac's edge to stunning country estates in Maryland and Virginia. Enchanting houses from the 18th and 19th centuries have been preserved or updated for today's lifestyles. Contemporary residences are bold and new, with sleek, streamlined interiors. Each designer has created a home that encompasses comfort, style and homeowner individuality.

The collaboration between designers and clients is how limits are pushed, rules are broken, and lifestyles are reflected in timeless elegance or period detail. The carefully orchestrated process may start with a swatch of fabric, an antique lamp or an empty room, but it must always include careful listening on the part of the designer, and openness on the part of the client.

The highly regarded interior designers and decorators showcased in this book each have the ability to bring color, texture, form and function to your home. Most are widely published; many are award winning. All have the ability to help incorporate personal style into a spectacular home to call your very own.

Enjoy!

Kathryn Newell

Kathryn Newell
Senior Associate Publisher

Photograph by Carol Bates

DESIGNER: Lisa Bartolomei, Bartolomei and Company, *Page 17*

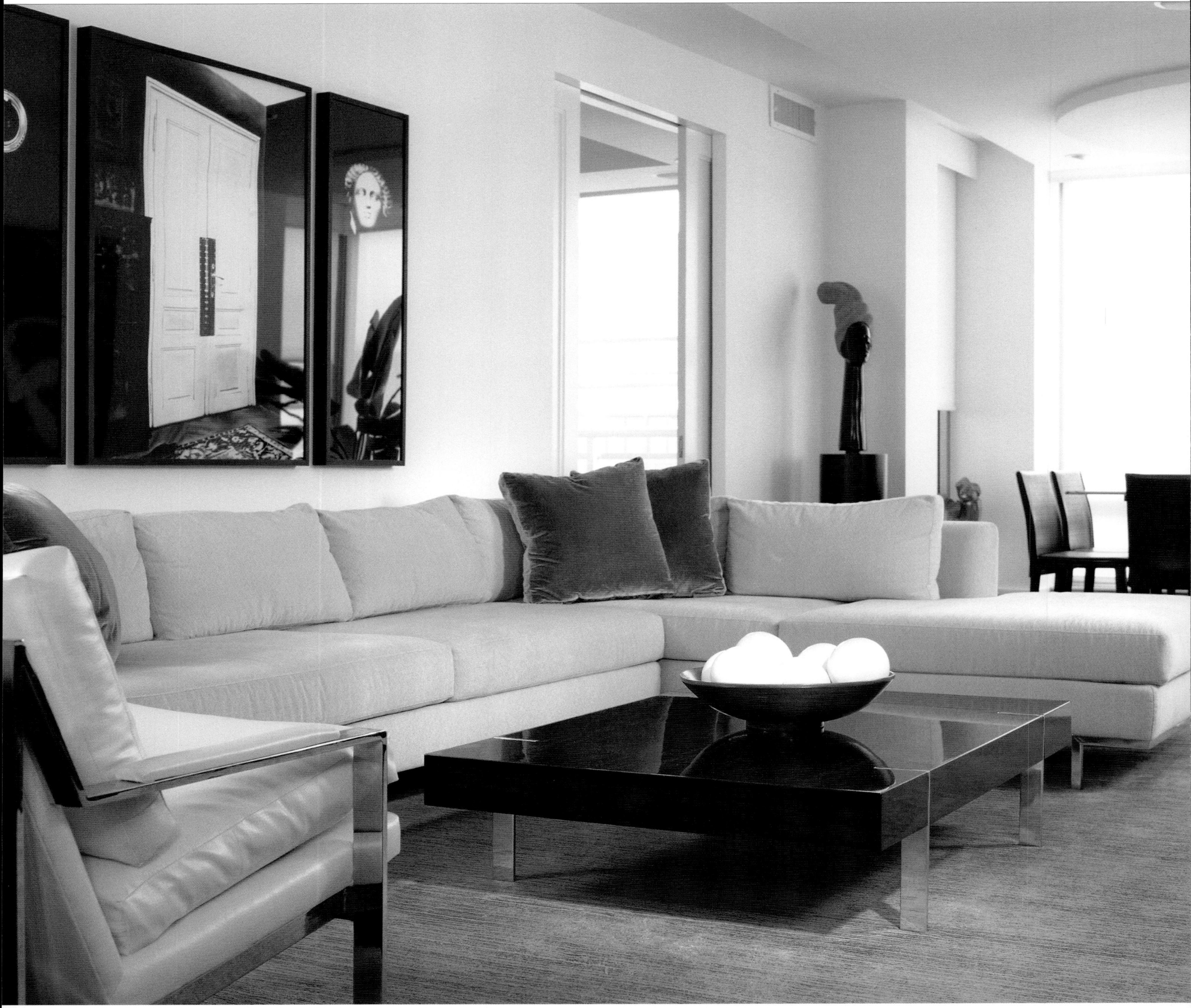

table of contents

DESIGNER: Kelly Flocks, Antony Childs, Inc., *Page 43*

DESIGNER: Lisa Adams, Adams Design, Inc., *Page 11*

DESIGNER: Marcia Bogert Hayman, Marcia Bogert Hayman, Inc., *Page 55*

Washington, D.C.

Lisa **Adams**

ADAMS DESIGN, INC.

Lisa Adams' passion for the applied side of art and design began with her nursery school educational experiences in the museums of New York. Her two favorite places to visit were the spinning color wheel in the Metropolitan Museum of Art that demonstrated color interaction, and the Products by Design room at the Museum of Modern Art.

In one of the early classes of women at Yale, Lisa followed a serious track through school, going on to earn an MBA from Columbia University's Graduate School of Business. Jobs followed in finance where she focused on corporate planning and strategic development. Throughout, she maintained her interest in art and design. When her son was born in 1987, the break in her schedule gave her the freedom to act on her interests and take a course in drafting. The experience was an epiphany. She went on to complete an undergraduate degree in interior design, working for an architecture firm for a number of years before launching her Washington, D.C. firm in 1998.

The career shift, as Lisa likes to point out, is not as dramatic as it may seem. Design and finance both involve problem solving and deal with solving simultaneous equations. A project may have, for example, five different constraints that must be met. When one solves for all of them, a result is achieved.

LEFT:
A master bedroom with a contemporary tone.
Photograph by Alan Dynerman, Architect

In design Adams solves for aesthetic and function. Function might break down into spatial circulation or into textiles where patterns and textures work in an environment with young children and dogs.

Design for Lisa is a concrete exercise, not something that happens in the abstract. Everyone has a point of view, and the challenge is discovering and revealing that position to determine what the client wants to elicit from their environment. She first addresses the space, learning how her clients live and how they experience their surroundings, how they function in it, and how the layout can better mirror their needs.

Lisa strives not to embrace a signature style. Instead she focuses on understanding the client and designing for their unique needs. What is their taste, what colors do they respond to, are they colorblind, how do they use their space? What do they do when they entertain, what will their space suggest about them? Each client brings different problems and concerns that need to be addressed with unique solutions.

Pieces with clean lines, whether in a traditional, transitional or contemporary setting, are essential to Lisa's aesthetic. She likes to mix antiques with this clean-lined style to add history, ornament and complexity. Elements of interest are essential throughout the space. From the dining room table, for example, each guest should enjoy a view of something wonderful.

ABOVE LEFT:
A master bedroom as seen through the four-poster bed. The gardens can be viewed through the windows.
Photograph by Peter Leach

ABOVE RIGHT:
A powder room for a client who is a voracious reader. The wallpaper's images of books are echoed in the display of miniature books on the shelf.
Photograph by Peter Leach

FACING PAGE:
A contemporary living room washed in color.
Photograph by Alan Dynerman, Architect

Lisa recently took on the reinvention of a historic hunting shack on Cape Cod's National Seashore. When the client bought the structure it was a typical hunting cabin—dark, wood paneling and orange shag carpeting, and no running water or electricity. Lisa transformed it into an upbeat beach cottage where all the elements work equally well indoors or out. A pile of three mattresses covered in indoor/outdoor fabric make a sofa but it can be disassembled and dragged onto the deck or into the sand to accommodate the many children who are overnight guests. A picnic table functions as the dining table. Bright beach colors—lime green and aqua—complement the views of sky, sand and water. Designer's Guild sheets in orange and pink bring unexpected color and elegance to the bunk room.

While Lisa works on projects in cities throughout the country—a residence in Huntsville, Alabama recently won an AIA Merit award in Architecture—she loves the environment in Washington. She may have a client in Georgetown who wants to do a traditional Federal-style house, or someone who's just bought a loft; a young person starting out who's a federal employee with limited means, or a house in the suburbs with four kids and two dogs. The hugely variable market is a perfect fit for her mutable and functional sensibilities.

ABOVE:
A modern bathroom with a soaking tub, an open shower and an island sink. Pebble tiles on the floor contrast with the silk draperies.
Photograph by Lydia Cutter

FACING PAGE LEFT:
A lady's sitting room. Colors evoke the flowering crab apple tree outside the French doors.
Photograph by Peter Leach

FACING PAGE RIGHT:
A window seat nook; a place to curl up to read, to nap or to enjoy one's solitude.
Photograph by Peter Leach

More about Lisa ...

WHAT DISTINGUISHES YOUR APPROACH TO DESIGN?
An aesthetic that respects functionality.

WHAT ONE CONSISTENT ELEMENT HAS BEEN WITH YOU THROUGHOUT YOUR CAREER?
My rooms are simple with clean lines. Forms speak for themselves without embellishment.

WHAT PERSONAL INDULGENCE CAN YOU NOT LIVE WITHOUT?
I'm an incurable collector of books. I love to read fiction, and finish 10 books a month. I am currently reading Joan Didion's memoir, *The Year of Magical Thinking*.

ADAMS DESIGN, INC.
Lisa Adams
1521 Wisconsin Avenue Northwest
Washington, D.C. 20007
202.333.1220
www.adamsdesign.com

Lisa **Bartolomei**

BARTOLOMEI AND COMPANY

Lisa Bartolomei, founder of design firm Bartolomei and Company, practiced commercial interior design concentrating on a variety of projects, including restaurants, hotels, banks, retail stores, law offices and health facilities for 10 years before making the move to residential interiors. Her strong desire to make an impact on individuals' lives led her to create the firm in 1986, and she has been improving her clients' lives ever since. Committed to helping people find happiness in their home and making the interior space work for them, her keen artistic eye and design expertise blossoms with each project she completes.

"Design is all about my clients." Lisa's incredible ability to listen has given her a reputation as a designer who "listens between the lines." Making every effort to get to know her clients before launching the design process, she goes through image after image with her clients, accompanies them on shopping trips and spends time talking with them to ascertain what they love and also what they hate about different aspects of design. She also works within her clients' budgets with a keen understanding that design priorities shift on a client-to-client basis. Her innate ability to listen, coupled with her intuitive understanding of client

needs, enables her to convey what her clients want before they can conceive it themselves.

Lisa prefers that her work reflect who the client is and not who the designer is. "I want each of my clients' homes to look as if they have been collecting things over a lifetime, not as if a designer has just stepped in to make things perfect." She gathers every bit of information possible to determine how her clients like to live and then she uses her expertise to create a better lifestyle for them. Lisa truly enjoys the problem-solving element of design, often creating custom pieces of furniture as well

ABOVE:
A component system from Italy creates a sleek and dynamic powder room, complemented by a custom mirror and pearlized Venetian plaster walls.
Photograph by Geoffrey Hodgdon

FACING PAGE:
The contemporary apartment is ideal for a client whose business life is demanding and chaotic. Coming home to this environment helps her completely relax.
Photograph by Geoffrey Hodgdon

as redesigning the architectural elements within the spaces; all of which gives her clients unique, comfortable, beautiful and highly usable environments.

Creating a total environment is a unique task for each client with whom she works. When a client called on Lisa to design her Ritz-Carlton penthouse, it was her objective to create a peaceful space that would help minimize clutter and maximize calm for this client living with Attention Deficit Disorder. Decorating the space with accents from her client's world travels, she kept the environment monochromatic while focusing on symmetry and structure in order to provide a serene, orderly feeling for her client.

TOP LEFT:
For a couple whose tastes ranged from contemporary to traditional, Lisa used classic shapes and traditional materials. The sofa and coffee table are Bartolomei designs.
Photograph by Geoffrey Hodgdon

BOTTOM LEFT:
For the dining room, Lisa found vintage Agostini sconces in London, a Sabino Pendant light in New York and designed the mirror and buffet.
Photograph by Geoffrey Hodgdon

FACING PAGE:
For the bedroom, Lisa created a sumptuous bed using silk charmeuse pillows and duvet. The watery blue colors reflect their beautiful river view.
Photograph by Geoffrey Hodgdon

Lisa provides this same personalized service for each client. In order to offer these personalized interiors that have become her hallmark, Lisa travels on buying trips to London, Paris, Venice, New York, Atlanta, New Orleans and California, providing her clients with unique furnishings and artwork at excellent prices. While based in Washington, D.C., her work reaches the global scale; she has completed projects in Jordon, Paris, Florida, Bermuda, New York City, The Hamptons, San Francisco and numerous residences in the Washington, D.C. area. As Bartolomei and Company grows, so does their reach; Lisa has been featured in the pages of numerous publications, including *Interior Design* magazine, *The Washington Post* and on the screens of televisions across the country on "Good Morning America" and "ABC News" with John Harter.

ABOVE LEFT:
For the "What's Modern Now" Showhouse in D.C., Lisa used a mixture of '40s-inspired furniture, magenta walls and cream upholstery highlighted with a Pucci print throw. Rose photo by Geoffrey Hodgdon.
Photograph by Geoffrey Hodgdon

ABOVE RIGHT:
The gentleman's study includes a custom-designed desk positioned for a bird's eye view. The deep russet walls serve as a warm backdrop for the art and furnishings.
Photograph by Geoffrey Hodgdon

FACING PAGE TOP:
This striking entrance was designed to feature the owners' painting. The waterfall feature to the left adds natural light to the master bath shower behind it.
Photograph by Geoffrey Hodgdon

FACING PAGE BOTTOM:
These anigre walls contain storage from top to bottom. They create a dramatic display for sculpture as well as a rich entry into the private library.
Photograph by Geoffrey Hodgdon

Q&A
More about Lisa ...

WHAT IS A SINGLE THING YOU WOULD DO TO BRING A DULL HOUSE TO LIFE?
Better use of color, architectural focal points, window structure and lighting are sure to bring a dull house to life.

WHO HAS HAD THE BIGGEST INFLUENCE ON YOUR CAREER?
Helene Giafferi, a friend of mine and dealer of fine art in Paris. She took me by the hand and led me through homes and auction houses in Europe, further educating my eye for design.

HAVE YOU BEEN PUBLISHED IN ANY NATIONAL OR REGIONAL PUBLICATIONS?
I've been published in many publications. My work was featured on the cover of *Country Inns* and in the pages of the *Washington Business Journal*, *The Washington Post Magazine*, *Washingtonian Magazine*, *Style*, *Interior Design*, *Home & Design* magazine, *Chesapeake Home* and *Washington Spaces* magazine.

WHAT PERSONAL INDULGENCE DO YOU SPEND THE MOST MONEY ON?
Travel; I love Italy and France, and I couldn't live without New York. It is a place like no other and a virtual candy store for any designer.

NAME ONE THING MOST PEOPLE DON'T KNOW ABOUT YOU.
I am actually rather shy. Design is a great fit for me because I am able to come out of my shell working with people and their homes.

BARTOLOMEI AND COMPANY
Lisa Bartolomei
3209 M Street Northwest
Washington, D.C. 20007
202.965.7667
f: 202.338.5221
www.bartolomeiandcompany.com

Lynda Huguely Camalier

LYNDA HUGUELY CAMALIER, ASID

A philosophy to which Lynda Camalier has always subscribed is "Never say never!" Moving effortlessly through any style, Lynda eludes an idiosyncratic flavor and in doing so is able to completely immerse herself in her client's design sensibilities. She is adamant about incorporating her client's choices into each project, predicating the creation of spaces that become much more than beautifully adorned, but also serve as a unique function of her client's lifestyle.

Flexibility is the key to a room that inspires and repetition is something that Lynda absolutely will not allow in her design. Expertly mixing color, texture and pattern while varying formality with scale and shade give her interiors an unequalled personality and a perfectly relaxed approach to sophisticated elegance. Art and accessories display a mindful, collected look and are mingled amongst remarkable finishes and unforgettable furnishings to form environments that are more soothing than strict.

A Washingtonian by birth, Lynda has spent her entire life in the D.C. area and began her design firm there 27 years ago, a business which is small but bustling. She decided to go into business for herself so that she could exercise her own choice on project selection. She began her first job as a commercial designer only a

LEFT:
This sunny yellow sunroom, which features long windows and doors, brings the outside in. The sunroom serves as an extension to the formal living room as well. Soft-colored fabrics mixed with ebony-toned furniture and a chocolate ottoman further complement the room.
Photograph by Bob Narod, Photographer, LLC

month after her college graduation and since that time, she has established herself as an accomplished and prestigious designer who is able to push the envelope while keeping tradition as the driving force.

Lynda's remarkable talents have been showcased in numerous publications including *Mid Atlantic Country, Renovation Style, Better Homes & Gardens, Washingtonian, The Washington Post* and *The Washington Post Magazine*. Additionally, she was honored with a room in the National Symphony Orchestra Decorators' Showhouse twice, most recently in 2002 at The Houghton Mansion, a sprawling Georgian Revival-style brick home with almost 50 rooms.

ABOVE:
This monochromatic kitchen uses a mix of textures and tones.
Photograph by Bob Narod, Photographer, LLC

FACING PAGE:
This formal gentlemen's dressing/bathroom is lush with details.
Photograph by Gordon Beall

ABOVE:
A lady's en suite bath area of simplicity and beauty creates an intimate escape with warm-colored walls.
Photograph by Gordon Beall

Q&A

More about Lynda ...

WHAT DO YOU LIKE MOST ABOUT BEING A DESIGNER IN THE D.C. AREA?
There are antique and art dealers everywhere, but those I come across in this area are genuinely great people. I have so many inspirations here; lots of great friends who are also amazing designers and a wonderful resource.

ON WHAT PERSONAL INDULGENCE DO YOU SPEND THE MOST MONEY?
Dishware of all kinds: ironstone, earthenware, pottery, porcelains and ceramics, all old and new.

TELL US SOMETHING THAT PEOPLE MIGHT NOT KNOW ABOUT YOU.
I am always trying new art of all kinds. Last fall it was knitting and this fall I am going to try my hand at ceramics and pot throwing.

WHAT IS YOUR FAVORITE THING TO DO FOR RELAXATION?
I cherish spending time in the country with my family.

WHAT BOOK ARE YOU CURRENTLY READING?
My reading list is comprised of two books, *Angle of Repose* by Wallace Stegner and *The Other Boleyn Girl* by Philippa Gregory. Both are monumental works of fiction of more than 500 pages each. (And if they say anything at all about Lynda, it is that she certainly isn't afraid of a challenge.)

LYNDA HUGUELY CAMALIER, ASID
Lynda Huguely Camalier
1629 K Street Northwest, Suite 1200
Washington, D.C. 20006
202.365.6417
f: 202.234.9292

ABOVE TOP:
This spa invites wonderful light and features a pair of wire chairs.
Photograph by Gordon Beall

ABOVE BOTTOM:
This sitting room, pleasantly arranged in the middle of the suite, captures the cclor and soft ambiance found throughout the suite.
Photograph by Gordon Beall

Lee **DeFord**
Edna **Sharp Gross**

DEFORD SHARP INTERIORS

Among Washington's top designers, Lee DeFord and Edna Sharp Gross are recognized as masters of classic interiors—traditional with a contemporary twist. Lee and Edna established their design partnership nearly 25 years ago and today their firm, DeFord Sharp Interiors, is well known for its elegant and sophisticated, yet inviting and uncompromisingly comfortable residential work.

Over the years, Lee and Edna have fulfilled a wide variety of projects, all reflecting the common goal of easy modern living and aesthetic appreciation. Edna suggests they have "evolved to cleaner, less complicated, but more eclectic designs." Lee says they "work without formula." And, without exception, they work closely with clients to fully comprehend their requirements and ensure results will reflect their interests and lifestyles.

Lee and Edna combine skillful planning and expert project management to provide clients with complete service, from feasibility to installation. They achieve the best results in all aspects of a project—from the interior architecture and the custom furnishings, to the collections of antiques and fine art—by uniting their individual strengths. "We aim to work as one mind," Edna says. The duo executes each

project with dedication to the highest standards of quality. "We are always mindful to work strictly within the parameters of prescribed timeframes and budgetary resources," shares Lee.

DeFord Sharp's personalized high-quality service keeps clients coming back. Most new clients come from past or existing client referrals. Although the majority of the firm's work is in the Washington metro region, Lee and Edna have also worked throughout the United States and Europe. They often find themselves traveling for the right creative challenges. And, along the way, their inspired achievements have earned them acclaim as a proven expert resource for unparalleled top-quality interior design.

ABOVE:
The calming neutral color scheme, furniture with clear-cut lines, uncluttered display of fine art and accessories and freshness of the crisp linens all contribute to the soothing appeal of this light and airy bedroom.
Photograph by Gordon Beall

FACING PAGE:
The classical and the contemporary fuse in this sophisticated living room where Far East elements serve to heighten the vitality of the decoration. The supremely comfortable seating is arranged for intimacy. The overall effect is timeless elegance.
Photograph by Gordon Beall

From large-scale architectural commissions to more modest refurbishment projects, whether a new construction residence, a recreational home, or a historical property, DeFord Sharp's record of inspired interiors is impressive. Their projects have attracted the news media and have appeared in various publications, including *ChesapeakeHome*, *Renovation Style*, *Traditional Home*, and *The Washington Post*.

ABOVE:
Casual yet stylish, this gracious room maximizes livability and comfort at a Rehoboth Beach property. It is an inviting, harmonious place for quiet solitude as well as gatherings of family and friends. Notably, the substantial beams, like the fireplace mantle, were accentuated with a faux-painted finish for greater presence.
Photograph by Anne Gummerson and Curtis Martin

FACING PAGE TOP:
In a Glover Park home, this modest-sized dining room thinks big and gives large comfort. The tall windows along one wall and the ample openings onto other rooms give the illusion of spaciousness. And the antique furnishings, including an 18th-century French oval wine tasting table, lend mellow character and warmth.
Photograph by Gordon Beall

FACING PAGE BOTTOM:
An arrangement of decorative accents of contrasting forms and textures, as shown on this table, can contribute to the visual dynamics of any room.
Photograph by Gordon Beall

Q&A

More about Lee & Edna ...

WHAT IS THE MOST UNIQUE/IMPRESSIVE/BEAUTIFUL HOME YOU'VE BEEN INVOLVED WITH? WHY?

We endeavor to achieve uniqueness and beauty in all our work and appreciate each project for its own challenges; however, we are most impressed by the projects that involve extraordinary collections of exquisite antiques and fine art. It is a special delight to work with enthusiastic collectors. Fortunately, we have been privileged to work with some of the most passionate and knowledgeable of collectors.

WHAT ONE ELEMENT OF STYLE OR PHILOSOPHY HAVE YOU STUCK WITH FOR YEARS THAT STILL WORKS FOR YOU TODAY?

We shun the artificial and trendy and instead draw our design inspirations from the classic and authentic. For us, it is essential to plan properly—nothing is left to chance. We believe only quality lasts. The details in our work expose our creative depths.

WHAT IS THE HIGHEST COMPLIMENT YOU'VE RECEIVED PROFESSIONALLY?

The highest compliment is the praise we receive for the personal commitment given to clients and our inexhaustible dedication to a project.

DEFORD SHARP INTERIORS
Lee DeFord
Edna Sharp Gross
1651 Wisconsin Avenue Northwest
Washington, D.C. 20007
202.333.3783
f: 202.625.6397
www.DeFordSharpInteriors.com

Noami **DeVore**

NOAMI DEVORE INTERIORS, LLC

As a child, Noami DeVore enjoyed creating beautiful spaces and was consistently active in the creative arts; however, as a young adult she delved into comparative literature and Russian language with the assumption that her future career would involve writing or communications. As her collegiate studies neared completion, the future was suddenly upon her, and Noami found herself undeniably drawn towards the field of interior design. Redefining her career path was not an easy decision, but she knew she needed to pursue her dream; and she has never looked back.

Working with legendary designer Thomas Pheasant for five years during the blossoming phase of her career, Noami was exposed to the highest levels of skill and creativity and the endless possibilities of customization. Thomas Pheasant gave her an incredible opportunity by sharing his knowledge and working with her to cultivate the design skills for which she has become so acclaimed. She learned to approach each project with an open mind, as an artist approaches a blank canvas. Each detail in an interior is equivalent to a brush stroke; alone it may be seemingly insignificant, but it adds a depth and richness that is crucial to the end result. The final product is only as good as the sum of its parts.

LEFT:
Custom-designed built-ins provide both form and function for this bright, casual family-oriented living space.
Photograph by Sora DeVore

This strong foundation of knowledge paired with Noami's natural design instinct inspired the young designer to open her own studio, Noami DeVore Interiors, in the fall of 2003.

Noami was quickly recognized for her strong understanding of color theory and her ability to create clean contemporary spaces while maintaining a sense of warmth and comfort. Believing no two projects are the same because each client is individual in their wants and needs, Noami enjoys the challenge of working as a "translator" for her clients, striving to make their definition of an ideal home come to life in a clear vision. Her approach makes the process enjoyable and the result

rewarding for Noami and her clients. "I consider it an honor to shape the style of someone's home; our home is our sanctuary, so it is not a task I take lightly."

Noami, a native Washingtonian, finds that designing in her hometown gives her the opportunity to observe the exciting growth and evolution of the city. "Change is good," she says. I often tell my clients as they contemplate a new vision for their home, 'It's okay to let go of who you were, and explore who you are now.' It's a lesson that can be applied in all aspects of life. I did it, and look where I am today!"

Q&A

More about Noami ...

WHO HAS HAD THE BIGGEST INFLUENCE ON YOUR CAREER?
Thomas Pheasant's friendship and tutelage has been priceless in defining my career.

WHAT IS THE ONE THING YOU WOULD DO TO BRING A DULL HOUSE TO LIFE?
Choose an accent color and incorporate it throughout the house with paint and decorative accessories.

WHAT IS A FAVORITE PIECE IN YOUR OWN HOME?
It is a 1950's Asian-inspired, green lacquer and floral motif cabinet which I purchased from an antique store in Georgetown. It caught my eye because I had never seen anything like it. It was the first piece of "real" furniture I bought for myself, and I cherish it.

NOAMI DEVORE INTERIORS, LLC
Noami DeVore
4574 Indian Rock Terrace Northwest
Washington, D.C. 20007
202.237.6283

ABOVE TOP:
A combination of textures and interesting eclectic finds mixed with fresh colors and clean lines allows this living room to entertain the eye while remaining uncluttered.
Photograph by Sora DeVore

ABOVE BOTTOM:
Color photographs by Sora DeVore bring pop and personality into this casually elegant dining room. Dining chairs upholstered in powder blue ultra suede make the space kid-friendly and worry free.
Photograph by Sora DeVore

FACING PAGE LEFT:
Contemporary yellow dupioni silk lanterns illuminate this eclectic, comfortable dining space.
Photograph by Sora DeVore

FACING PAGE RIGHT:
This foyer sets the tone for a fun, chic family home. Vintage yellow ceramic lamps are paired with an 18th-century Chinese console. "Pussy Willow" photograph by Sora DeVore.
Photograph by Sora DeVore

Mary Douglas Drysdale

DRYSDALE INC.

M ary Douglas Drysdale grew up in the shadow of Monticello, continually influenced by the ever present spirit of architect/president Thomas Jefferson. It is her strong belief that the connections and transitions between art, architecture and decoration must be seamless. The Drysdale approach begins with clarity of vision. Her approach and abilities encompass a broad skill set. Initially drawn to architecture, her passion took her to Paris at an early age where she embarked on a self-styled, three-year "Grand Tour" to study the great houses of Europe and the classical styles.

Architectural studies were then followed by schooling in Interior Design/Environmenta Design and Industrial Design. The emphasis at Drysdale is to conceive of and implement complete, holistic projects reflecting the personalities and lifestyles of the clientele. Interior planning, decoration, furniture design, construction management, art selection and the integration of up-to-date technologies into the building envelope differentiate the abilities of this firm from others.

A totally consumed problem solver who never limits her palette, Mary Douglas Drysdale's oeuvre is a testament to her ability to work in all styles from period to up-to-the-moment modern—rustic to urban sophisticated.

LEFT:
Residence of a contemporary glass collector. All furnishings designed by Mary Douglas Drysdale.
Photograph by Andrew Lautman

"In our office it is really about individually-tailored designs, not what we did on the last job. We mold our solutions to the program and style of each client, with the presence of the architecture always respected." While well known for her European approach, Ms. Drysdale is also a master at adapting her style to any environment. She counts among her many strengths the ability to take traditional building aspects and update them to meet the modern client's needs.

Most of Mary's clients remain so for life—an honor and example of her innate ability to engage lay individuals in the design process. The recognition of her work is international and her design accomplishments impressive. Numerous publications and awards recognize these accomplishments. Forty-seven cover stories and hundreds of articles chronicle her career. These publications include *Architectural Digest, Southern Accents, Veranda, House Beautiful, House and Garden, Departures, This Old House* (who selected her as one of the top 40 building experts in the United States) and others. *House Beautiful* selected Mary Douglas Drysdale for five years running as one of the top 100 designers in America, and in 2000 she was named one of the top practicing architects and designers in the United States by *Interiors* magazine. *Traditional Home* awarded her their coveted "Design Excellence Award," and *Dossier* magazine their first "House of the Year award."

In addition to her acclaim in print media, Ms. Drysdale is frequently invited to be a keynote speaker at different design centers and events around the country. A resident of Washington, D.C., she calls the nation's capital home but often pursues projects around the country.

ABOVE:
Eighteenth-century furniture and contemporary art.
Photograph by Peter Vitale

FACING PAGE:
A Beaux Arts-style townhouse enlivened by golden yellow tones.
Photograph by Peter Vitale

Q&A

More about Mary ...

WHAT IS THE HIGHEST COMPLIMENT YOU'VE RECEIVED PROFESSIONALLY?
A client said his vision of architecture had been enhanced by the experience of living in a house I designed.

WHO HAS HAD THE BIGGEST INFLUENCE ON YOUR CAREER?
Certainly Thomas Jefferson has had a huge influence. He was a man whose understanding of design was so complete and perfect—his oeuvre is timeless.

HOW WOULD YOU DESCRIBE YOUR PERSONAL STYLE?
Refined sensibility of classical thinking with a little bit of sassiness!

WHAT DO YOU ENJOY MOST ABOUT DOING BUSINESS IN THE D.C. AREA?
I like the power magnet the city holds; the city attracts many educated, interesting and exciting folks.

DRYSDALE INC.
Mary Douglas Drysdale
2026 R Street Northwest
Washington, D.C. 20009
202.588.0700
f: 202.588.8464

ABOVE:
A coastal property renovated by Mary Douglas Drysdale.
Photograph by Andrew Lautman

FACING PAGE:
An 18th-century Pennsylvania stone farmhouse.
Photograph by Andrew Lautman

Kelly flocks

ANTONY CHILDS, INC.

Antony Childs, Inc. was founded in Georgetown, Washington, D.C. in 1968 by Antony Childs, a nationally acclaimed and award-winning interior designer. Kelly Flocks worked with Mr. Childs for 12 years before assuming responsibility for the firm upon his death in 1994. Under Kelly's direction, Antony Childs, Inc. has continued Tony's tradition of achieving a comfortable approach to cosmopolitan lifestyles by combining smart space planning, color, antiques and fine art.

A native Washingtonian, Kelly Flocks earned her Bachelor of Fine Arts degree at American University. She worked both during her studies and after graduation with S. D. Jeffrey & Associates. One of the foremost design firms in the greater metropolitan Washington area, Jeffrey specialized in furnishing high-end model homes. There Kelly gained invaluable insight and experience into the constraints of completing projects within deadlines without compromising quality or aesthetic vision.

LEFT:
National Symphony Orchestra Decorators' Showhouse, Washington, D.C. The grand but comfortable library is focused around a collection of 19th-century antique furnishings including an English Regency gilded chair and mahogany screen with silk panels offset by a simple Japanese tatami mat.
Photograph by Harlan Hambright

After several years with Jeffrey, Kelly relocated to Philadelphia to work with Carl Steele & Associates, one of the city's premier design firms. Under Carl's tutelage Kelly developed her skills in authenticating fine art and rare antiques. Kelly's expertise in this area makes her a sought-after and unique talent in discovering and facilitating the placement of extraordinary pieces.

Published in *House & Garden, House Beautiful, The Washington Post, Veranda* and *Luxury Homes*, Antony Childs, Inc. has been recognized for its exquisite work by some of the finest design publications. Kelly's interiors are well proportioned and communicate understated elegance. The soothing style is comfortable, never fussy, resulting in fresh interiors that are as beautiful as they are livable. She persists in choosing ageless excellence over trends, believing that "anything that is good is good forever."

Well versed in many styles, Kelly moves comfortably within them as her clients' tastes dictate. She subscribes to the belief that every historical style, regardless of its individual merit, has contributed to the evolution of design, resulting in the rich heritage we have today.

Kelly truly loves being a part of creating beautiful spaces and enjoys scouting area shops for that one-of-a-kind piece to complete a design. With her broad knowledge of antiques and her adept eye for timeless pieces, Kelly is an expert at spotting just the right furnishings and accessories to complement her clients' lifestyles and preferences.

ABOVE:
The living room of a private residence combines the client's collection of French and English antiques with comfortable custom upholstered pieces and splashes of color to create a tranquil atmosphere.
Photograph by Gordon Beall

FACING PAGE:
National Symphony Orchestra Decorators' Showhouse, Washington, D.C. A grand foyer, featuring luxurious 18th-century English Regency and Georgian furniture and showcasing an abstract painting by Thorvald Hellesen, is made less formal with hand-stenciled sisal carpet. Walls are hand painted to resemble cut block limestone.
Photograph by Gordon Beall

ABOVE:
This 19th-century English Georgian-style master bedroom features a four-poster bed, European furniture and accents of floral chintz. The room is softened by a glowing palette.
Photograph by Gordon Beall

FACING PAGE TOP:
Campagna Center of Alexandria, Virginia Showhouse, outdoor loggia. This loggia brings the indoors outside with three painted iron grills to camouflage the windows; portieres to add softness; and versatile indoor/outdoor furniture with graceful lines. The liberal use of white cotton provides a peaceful and mellow retreat.
Photograph by Gordon Beall

FACING PAGE BOTTOM:
Campagna Center of Alexandria, Virginia Showhouse, outdoor loggia. Another view of the loggia reveals an 18th-century terracotta bust of Ceres and a hexagonal English stone table surrounded by a modern interpretation of classical Greek klismos chairs with scalloped natural linen slip covers.
Photograph by Gordon Beall

Q&A

More about Kelly …

ON WHAT PERSONAL INDULGENCE DO YOU SPEND THE MOST MONEY?
My tortoiseshell-box collection.

TELL US ONE THING PEOPLE MIGHT NOT KNOW ABOUT YOU.
I am fluent in Greek.

YOU WOULDN'T KNOW IT BUT MY FRIENDS WOULD TELL YOU I WAS…
An extra in a hit Hollywood movie!

WHO HAD THE BIGGEST INFLUENCE ON YOUR CAREER?
Carl Steele and Antony Childs.

ANTONY CHILDS, INC.
Kelly Flocks
1668 Wisconsin Avenue Northwest
Washington, D.C. 20007
202.337.1100
f: 202.333.0996
www.antonychildsinc.com

Jerry **Harpole**

HARPOLE ARCHITECTS, P.C.

With a Master of Architecture from Harvard University Graduate School of Design and training from the École des Beaux-Artes in France, Jerry Harpole's academic achievements speak for themselves and say volumes about Jerry himself. Not only is he an architect, but an exceptional interior designer as well, giving him the unique ability to truly design an environment from the outside in. Well known for attention to detail, elegant design and rich architectural details in his interiors, Jerry transcends boundaries with a subtle touch, mixing modern and traditional elements in a harmonious and very livable fusion.

Simplicity is a key element in Jerry's design. You won't find cluttered rooms filled with unnecessary accessories. Rather, he believes in editing to create a clean look, standing firm that the only thing that should be collected is art. With fresh palettes that always enhance the foreground, he draws on aspects of the environment, architecture and furnishings to create a transitional mix of traditional and modern that flows seamlessly.

Each project presents a different challenge and varying inspiration. From the setting to the personality of the client, Jerry draws most of his direction simply from conversations with his clients. Making sure that their needs are addressed, he then takes his design to the next level, building on the existing platform established through consistently open lines of communication. Careful not to imprint his vision as the process progresses, he takes time getting to know each client well, learning their likes and dislikes and ultimately involving them in choices that affect their everyday lives, which gives them ownership in the finished product.

ABOVE:
The art collection includes the original Victorian fireplace as the focal point of the living room, as a piece of art should be.
Photograph by Philip Schmidt

FACING PAGE:
This reinterpreted Victorian townhouse has an unexpected twist by transposing the use of red from the windows to all of the upholstery.
Photograph by Philip Schmidt

Establishing a conceptual direction, Jerry then begins to refine the design in which the rooms become backdrops for their owners' personalities as he manipulates the space to create a lifestyle experience through beautiful living. He enjoys testing his abilities and trying new things to keep his designs fresh and new.

Views of the home's exterior and how it relates to its surroundings are facets that Jerry is always considering. His keen eye for detail and his ability to bring ideas into tangible, elegant and chic spaces have afforded Harpole Architects, P.C., a reputation as one of the premier full-service design firms in the Washington, D.C. area for over 25 years. His design doctrine of "less is more" also translates into his business practices. Moving to D.C. after his college graduation, Jerry put his roots down, establishing his own firm in 1982.

Jerry always has several projects and there are so many that he loves, though he feels that his work is still growing and evolving. Like a painter, each masterpiece becomes greater and better through learning and doing. He loves the idea of constantly learning and has evolved as a designer and as a person quite significantly over the years.

ABOVE:
No matter how large or small, the kitchen is where everything happens; cooking, dining, lounging, working. Multiple functions with multiple colors!
Photograph by Philip Schmidt

FACING PAGE TOP:
The dining room, being the center of the house and life, is all about comfort and living. The warmth of the fireplace is enhanced by the use of a red mosaic glass tile surround and hearth from Waterworks.
Photograph by Philip Schmidt

FACING PAGE BOTTOM:
The vibrant color palette of the kitchen stimulates all senses, as does food.
Photograph by Philip Schmidt

Q&A

More about Jerry ...

IF YOU COULD ELIMINATE ONE ARCHITECTURAL BUILDING TECHNIQUE FROM THE WORLD, WHAT WOULD IT BE?
Victorian!

WHO HAS HAD THE BIGGEST INFLUENCE ON YOUR CAREER?
There are so, so many that it's hard to name just one. My clients are a major influence. They expect a lot, and I deliver.

WHAT DO YOU LIKE MOST ABOUT DOING BUSINESS IN D.C.?
Washington, D.C. has changed dramatically in the last five years. It's more urban and less traditional. Its residents are becoming more willing to do different things.

WHAT IS YOUR FAVORITE STYLE PERSONALLY?
A transitional mix of modern and traditional. And I love avant garde art!

HARPOLE ARCHITECTS, P.C.
Jerry Harpole
1413B Wisconsin Avenue Northwest
Washington, D.C. 20007
202.338.3838
f: 202.338.3832

ABOVE:
The variety of the green marble shapes and sizes, from slab to mosaics, used in the master bath creates a calm place to cleanse body, soul and mind.
Photograph by Philip Schmidt

FACING PAGE:
The soothing blue-green palette of the private master bedroom is a respite from the active reds used elsewhere.
Photograph by Philip Schmidt

Marcia Bogert **Hayman**

MARCIA BOGERT HAYMAN, INC.

An interior designer who was once a broker on Wall Street, Marcia Bogert Hayman's inherent love for design led her away from the busy streets of New York City to the fabulous homes of the Washington area. While working on Wall Street, Marcia found herself more interested in decorating the apartment she and her husband shared than dealing in stocks and bonds. It was perhaps by a stroke of fate that she became an interior designer; after she and her husband relocated to Washington, D.C., Marcia was busy decorating their Georgetown townhouse. It was on a visit to Lord & Taylor's interior design department that she overheard the well-known designer Antony Childs interviewing an applicant for an all-purpose position in his office. This position sounded much more appealing than the ones she had been interviewing for at Washington brokerage firms, so she approached Tony, asked him for an interview and landed the job.

After a few months of working in Tony's office, it became clear to Marcia that the design world was where she wanted to be—for good. Following her good friend Diana Kerns' (who is now a Boston-based interior designer) advice, she enrolled in classes at The American University. In addition to a Bachelor of Science degree in Political Science with a minor in Russian, Marcia went on to earn a second degree in Fine Arts with a concentration in interior design.

LEFT:
The living room of this large Wesley Heights Tudor-style home features walls covered in hand-woven silk, a Sam Gilliam acrylic painting, T'ang Dynasty figures on cabinetry shelves, a Robert Maplethorpe photograph on foyer wall, an 18th-century horse weathervane, a hand-painted Rose Tarlow coffee table and a custom-woven Elizabeth Eakins rug.
Photograph by Maxwell MacKenzie

LEFT:
The same living room shown on the two
previous pages gives the reader an alternate
fireplace view which includes a David Hockney
oil/pastel over the fireplace, custom andirons
and firescreen by the designer, Rose Tarlow
rachet-back chairs, hand-stenciled ceiling beams
and a custom red leather low table by the
designer.
Photograph by Maxwell MacKenzie

FACING PAGE:
The walls of this formal dining room are
hand-painted strie with pearlized leaf and
branch design. Stunning antiques including
late-Chippendale chairs circa 1780, a pair of
Hepplewhite sideboards with brass galleries
circa 1790, a 19th-century Venetian mirror
and 18th-century blanc de chine porcelain
vases each add beautiful authenticity to the
dining experience.
Photograph by Maxwell MacKenzie

Practicing as a designer at Tony Childs' firm, Marcia had the opportunity to study under the late designer and hone her design skills. During this time, she was also able to build firm client relationships. These relationships became so firm, in fact, that when Marcia attempted to step away from interior design to raise a family, her clients wouldn't allow it!

"One of my clients at the time, an attorney, told me, 'I'll set up your business for you. Of course you'll keep working.'" recalled Marcia. "All of my clients really wanted me to continue working on their projects. It just happened like that and I managed to do it all the way through while raising my children. I'm still doing it and I don't think I'll ever quit. I love my job."

Her love for her job is clearly evident in Marcia's quality of work. She strives in each project to make the house and its design about the client, not about her own preferences. Approaching each project with fresh ideas, she treats each home as a new venture, staying away from looks that have been previously done.

One of Marcia's greatest joys is creating environments in which her clients love to live. Recently, clients with whom she had been working for 28 years had a party for their son. During dinner, a short film montage of events was played for all the party-goers to watch and Marcia was thanked in the film for giving them a wonderful background to raise their family. To Marcia, this compliment embodied exactly what she strives to accomplish in her work.

"I have such great clients. I have worked with some for 30 years," the designer reminisced. "The line between client and friend becomes blurred at that point."

As a testament to her client relationships, most of Marcia's clients are referred to her by current or past clients who insist their friends must work with the outstanding designer. Clients aren't the only ones impressed with her work; Marcia has been featured on the cover of *The Washington Post*'s Fall Home Interior Design section and in many other magazines and newspapers.

ABOVE:
The living room of this Bethesda home features Italian textured wallcovering, alabaster and bronze ceiling fixtures with hand-engraved sienna borders along with a magnificent collection of treasures including: custom steel/brass firescreen, 19th-century bronze andirons depicting Zeus and Athena, Pat Steir acrylic painting, 18th-century Giovanni Battista Cipriani black and red chalk drawing and a collection of 18th-century tea caddies and boxes.
Photograph by Anne Gummerson

FACING PAGE TOP:
The living room of this Potomac home highlights a Sam Gilliam acrylic painting, celadon frescoed walls, F.J. Hakimian custom Oushak rug, period Art Deco lounge chairs and a natural cherry coffee table with inset copper planter.
Photograph by Maxwell MacKenzie

FACING PAGE BOTTOM:
This focal point of this dining room is a table imported from Italy with base of Roman travertine columns and glass top. The room also includes Dakota Jackson down-filled kid leather upholstered armchairs, an 18th-century Italian walnut buffet with black marble top, scavo glass candlesticks and a custom "Couche de Soleil" mirror of amber glass set in translucent resin.
Photograph by Maxwell MacKenzie

Q&A

More about Marcia ...

WHAT IS THE HIGHEST COMPLIMENT YOU'VE
RECEIVED PROFESSIONALLY?
I was delighted when a well-known photographer who
specializes in architecture and interior design called my
work "exquisite."

WHAT ONE PHILOSOPHY HAVE YOU STUCK WITH FOR
YEARS THAT STILL WORKS FOR YOU TODAY?
I make the house about the client, not about me. I don't
have one look I do over and over again.

WHO HAS HAD THE BIGGEST INFLUENCE ON
YOUR CAREER?
Early in my career, I was privileged to have the opportunity
to work with the late Tony Childs, one of Washington's
premier designers at that time. He was always my friend and
mentor and the only designer I would have ever hired to do
my own home.

MARCIA BOGERT HAYMAN, INC.
Marcia Bogert Hayman, ASID
4836 MacArthur Boulevard Northwest
Washington, D.C. 20007
202.337.7788

Gary **Lovejoy**

GARY LOVEJOY ASSOCIATES, INC.

Gary Lovejoy's favorite piece in his own home is a gilded Victorian mirror, a flea market find and a magnificent one at that. It is juxtaposed to the contemporary design in the rest of his home, standing out—much like Gary and his tremendous body of work.

The genius of Gary's designs lie in their simplicity. His interiors are clean, uncluttered, and always elegant, whether they are modern or traditional in style. The character of his work evolves from his design philosophy, the focus of which is the importance of the interior as it relates to the architecture of a space in scale, proportion and style. Gary believes in a contemporary approach that visually expands the interior through finely designed details, furnishings and color.

A native Washingtonian, Gary is energized by the unequaled character of the city. With access to the world's foremost art and architecture, the city provides a wonderful blend of an accommodating and livable style. Gary has the distinction of having watched the area transform into a modern scene amid unmistakable historical influences.

With a bachelor's degree in interior design from the University of Maryland, Gary has spent the last 36 years in the world of design. Formerly of Lovejoy-Maxwell & Associates, Inc., Gary established his own firm in 1983. Now a paragon of D.C. design, Gary Lovejoy Associates, Inc. has been involved in creating brilliant and ethereal interiors for his clients' luxury homes, summer retreats and pieds-à-terre from South Beach to Manhattan.

ABOVE:
The curved lines of the kidney sofa situated in the bay window make this client's living room environment very inviting. Textures of silk, linen and wool add warmth.
Photograph by Gordon Beall

FACING PAGE:
A library in a traditional architectural setting—simple and uncluttered. With the addition of B&B Italia and Brueton upholstery, the room sparkles with today's lifestyles. Sconces designed by Gary Lovejoy for David Iatesta.
Photograph by Gordon Beall

Gary's creative talents have achieved recognition within the design community. He has received the ASID Designer of Distinction award and the Washington Design Hall of Fame award. His work has been published in *House Beautiful, Southern Accents, The Washington Post, Luxury Homes of Washington* and *Traditional Home*.

ABOVE:
This vignette in a guest suite shows a triptych canvas by artist Randy Rosenburg resting on a Jean Michael Frank custom console table. An antique Asian chest-on-chest provides extra storage, and the 'wow' art gives a secluded space pizzazz.
Photograph by Gordon Beall

FACING PAGE:
Asian influences and bold art statements make this contemporary gentleman's study unique and expressive. Abstract painting by Howard Mehring from the Washington Color School; lighting by Holly Hunt; furnishings by Donghia and Holly Hunt.
Photograph by Gordon Beall

ABOVE LEFT:
Classic, romantic, and inspiring, the ladies bath for the Houghton Mansion NSO Decorators' Showhouse is an example of refined elegance.
Photograph by Gordon Beall

ABOVE RIGHT:
An imaginative architectural treatment to the hallway railing. It leads to the master bedroom in a Victorian townhouse at Logan Circle, opening space and enhancing light.
Photograph by Gordon Beall

FACING PAGE TOP:
Modern renovation of a `60's Ranch-style home. Light, spacious, and beautifully detailed, this gallery entry is adorned by a bronze sculpture by Lisa Scheer; hanging paper shade by StvdiumV. Architecture by Schick Goldstein Architects.
Photograph by Hoachlander Davis

FACING PAGE BOTTOM:
A Mies van der Rohe leather lounge mixes with an oversized Holly Hunt coffee table in this expansive living room overlooking the trees of Great Falls. Wool custom rug by Stark and wall canvas by Sam Gilliam.
Photograph by Hoachlander Davis

Q&A

More about Gary ...

IF YOU COULD ELIMINATE ONE BUILDING TECHNIQUE OR STYLE FROM THE WORLD, WHAT WOULD IT BE?
McMansions!

WHAT IS THE BEST PART OF BEING AN INTERIOR DESIGNER?
By far, I enjoy enriching the lives of others more than any other aspect of my job.

WHAT'S THE HIGHEST PROFESSIONAL COMPLIMENT YOU'VE RECEIVED?
Recently a client of 30 years said to me, "It's been a wonderful thing that you have given us and one that we have appreciated for many years: a Gary Lovejoy interior!"

ON WHAT DO YOU INDULGE IN YOUR PRIVATE LIFE?
Traveling and cars! I have been fascinated with cars since I was a child. I can remember being inspired by the models my brother used to build and spending hours drawing them. I still get all the car magazines.

NAME ONE THING PEOPLE MIGHT NOT KNOW ABOUT YOU.
I love to sing (not in public) and love classic and Latin jazz.

GARY LOVEJOY ASSOCIATES, INC.
Gary Lovejoy, ASID
4564 Indian Rock Terrace Northwest
Washington, D.C. 20007
202.333.5200
www.GaryLovejoy.com

Victoria **Neale**

VICTORIA NEALE INTERIORS, LLC

Interior design may be Victoria Neale's second career, but there is no doubt that design is her calling. After first earning a degree in economics and spending six years in the banking industry, she woke up one day and said, "It's time!" Returning to school at 29, she pursued her second degree in interior design, graduating at the age of 32.

After graduating, Victoria studied under established D.C. area designers, honing her design skills and then striking out on her own. She opened Victoria Neale Interiors almost eight years ago in the bustling design district. Since that time, Victoria has made quite a name for herself and her designs, garnering national attention. *House Beautiful* named her one of "America's Top 125 Interior Designers" two years running, while *Southern Accents* featured her in their annual lineup of emerging talent, "Four Under 40."

Widely recognized for her fresh combinations and fearless but sophisticated use of color, Victoria loves to mix it up with painted pieces, woods, metals, textures and patterns. To balance that mix, each space has carefully proportioned layouts and a strong connection to the architecture of the house.

A key characteristic in all of Victoria's projects is her use of color rather than beige as a neutral. By using warm tones like gold, yellow or green as the main color for a room, she creates a serene envelope for each space. Strong punches of color are saved for pillows, ottomans and accessories. The end result is a house that is warm and inviting, bathed in color and infused with a refined and elegant feel.

Victoria is quick to point out that it is important to stay away from trends. She urges clients to choose colors and pieces that they love. In addition, she works hard to involve clients in selections to make sure that the house reflects their tastes. After determining the furniture layouts, clients select fabrics that "speak" to them. These fabrics become the catalyst for the color direction of the project. The "neutral" for the walls and upholstery pieces is chosen, and the mix of textures, solids and color accents develops from there.

ABOVE:
The sculptural forms of the table, chairs and chandelier in this dining room are balanced by the willowy orchids painted by artist John Matthew Moore.
Photograph by Angie Seckinger

FACING PAGE:
The custom headboard in this bedroom creates the perfect place to curl up and read in bed. The beiges make for a serene sleeping space, and the punches of apple green keep things fresh.
Photograph by Angie Seckinger

The longer Victoria practices, the more exciting the design process becomes. She loves to be challenged by each unique client and interior. Her management background also brings practical skills to the table that are intrinsic to the design process and the completion of projects. Each project brings new client ideas, new issues to resolve and new spaces to transform.

ABOVE:
Warm beiges set the stage for the furniture and the view in the living room of this aerie apartment. Modern and traditional elements are mixed, but the more formal arrangement of the furniture keeps the space in balance.
Photograph by Angie Seckinger

FACING PAGE TOP:
An eclectic mix of furniture and a sea grass rug balance the formality of the settee in this living room.
Photograph by Michel Arnaud

FACING PAGE BOTTOM:
Dorset Cream paint from Farrow & Ball with window treatments to match make this family room cozy and inviting.
Photograph by Michel Arnaud

Q&A

More about Victoria ...

WHAT COLOR BEST DESCRIBES YOU AND WHY?
I absolutely love orange! Orange is a word that scares people, but the family of colors is huge and gorgeous. Rooms done in tones of tangerine, pumpkin, saffron and persimmon are always welcoming, inviting and warm.

HOW DO YOU BEGIN THE DESIGN PROCESS?
I always start with furniture plans for each room. That gives each space a balance of scale, and that's where I begin to develop the vision for the project.

WHAT IS YOUR FAVORITE STYLE PERSONALLY?
It is somewhere between modern and traditional. My roots are in the traditional; I love historic architecture and have a traditional approach to furniture layouts. My use of color, though, is more modern. I like fresh combinations that are just a little bit surprising!

DO YOU FEEL LIKE YOUR WORK IS STILL EVOLVING?
My work is evolving absolutely every day. I learn new ways to see things from my clients, new ways to achieve my vision from the vendors I work with, and that's one of the most exciting aspects of my job. I would get bored giving the same "look" to each client.

VICTORIA NEALE INTERIORS, LLC
Victoria Neale
6120 Broad Branch Road Northwest
Washington, D.C. 20015
202.244.8410
f: 202.244.0019
www.victorianealeinteriors.com

Thomas **Pheasant**

THOMAS PHEASANT, INC.

Thomas Pheasant, a fourth-generation Washingtonian, is one of D.C.'s most highly respected and widely published interior designers. His work has been featured many times in *Architectural Digest, House Beautiful, House & Garden, Elle Décor* and *Southern Accents*. Among his many awards and achievements, Thomas was honored to have received the 1997 Andrew Martin International Designer of the Year award in London.

Washington, D.C. has been a great influence on Thomas's design point of view, supporting his creativity with the classical influence that is so prevalent in its architecture. Splitting his time between his home in Washington and his apartment in Paris, he surrounds himself with constant inspiration, believing there is simply so much to be said for the juxtaposition of old and new. With the restoration of antiquity comes inspiration for neoteric ideas that this noteworthy designer finds quite invigorating.

This doctrine is a defining element in Thomas's design sensibilities. Using classical expressions of the past to articulate something new, while always keeping in mind classicism and stylistic consistency, he creates an organic flow with strong forms and uncomplicated silhouettes. Working exhaustively to ensure that the

LEFT:
Simple upholstery, fine antiques and select furnishings designed by Thomas Pheasant work together, creating an inviting mix for this Washington library.
Photograph by Gordon Beall

architectural aspects of a project are accurate and precise, he then elevates the design by creating simple palettes in subtly varying shades, giving the room its richness and conveying a sense of calm that opens the environment to things like artwork and accessories. Finessing the details, Thomas completes each space with beautiful furnishings, tactile fabrics, simple palettes and plenty of antiques and paintings. His love for designing and creating unique furniture for his clients has brought him to the attention of national furniture companies. He has designed furniture collections for both Baker and McGuire under his signature—a signature built on simplicity, comfort and architectural inspiration

that allows him to move from traditional to modern interiors with ease. He has had the luxury of fulfilling his ideas and evolving his craft through the cumulative influences of his diverse clientele.

ABOVE:
A client's love for red inspired the warm monochromatic palette for this D.C. sitting room. By utilizing various shades of one color, the room becomes "neutralized," allowing the art and collections to become the focus of the room.
Photograph by Gordon Beall

FACING PAGE LEFT:
Sculptural silhouettes, classical elements and careful editing mark both the furnishings and interiors by Thomas Pheasant. The game table, chairs and light fixture are all designs by Thomas Pheasant.
Photograph by Gordon Beall

FACING PAGE RIGHT:
A small dining niche brings a warm modern elegance to the Washington kitchen.
Photograph by Gordon Beall

ABOVE:
Comfort and practicality directed the selections for this Maryland family room. The armchairs and ottomans by the fireplace are from the Thomas Pheasant for McGuire Collection.
Photograph by Gordon Beall

FACING PAGE LEFT:
Art, accessories and furnishings are carefully selected to work together. The simplest objects can often create the most elegant results.
Photograph by Gordon Beall

FACING PAGE RIGHT:
A romantic tone is set by this watery palette enhanced by sunlight and custom furnishings inspired by the 1940s. Tassel chairs by Thomas Pheasant.
Photograph by Gordon Beall

More about Thomas ...

WHAT IS THE MOST UNIQUE, BEAUTIFUL OR IMPRESSIVE HOME YOU'VE BEEN INVOLVED WITH AND WHY?

All of them; I only take on projects that I am greatly interested in doing. What I am working on at the time is the design that excites me. I could never say that one of my designs was more unique or beautiful than another; it would be like choosing a favorite child.

TELL US ONE THING THAT PEOPLE MIGHT NOT KNOW ABOUT YOU.

I would love to teach one day.

WHAT INDULGENCE DO YOU SPEND THE MOST MONEY ON?

Travel! When I was younger my focus was working and building my company. Now I make time to travel and open myself to the different cultures of the world. It inspires my work and keeps me energized.

WHAT COLOR BEST DESCRIBES YOU AND WHY?

My work and travel demands are great, so I like to surround myself in neutral palettes. A neutral setting combined with light, art and flowers is the best therapy for an active urban lifestyle.

THOMAS PHEASANT, INC.
Thomas Pheasant
1029 33rd Street Northwest
Washington, D.C. 20007
202.337.6596
f: 202.342.3941
www.thomaspheasant.com

Photograph by Rhoda Baer

Lorra **Rivers**
LR DESIGNS

Lorra Rivers, founder of LR Designs, was fortunate enough to know from a very young age that design was her calling. As a child, her parents nurtured her creative side by giving her pottery wheels and weaving looms instead of Barbie dolls. By high school, she was drafting and preparing for a career in design. After studying interior design and architecture in college, she immediately launched into her design career, never looking back.

Today, Lorra establishes a close rapport with her clients to ensure that their fundamental design needs are met and their most colorful desires are fulfilled. Believing that good design is a harmonious blending of shape, texture, color, proper scale and proportion, she finds great satisfaction in exposing her clients to these elements. "I love to take an environment my clients find challenging and transform it into a dramatic yet functional space. When I've convinced a client to reach outside the box and be open to new ideas, I'm halfway there."

ABOVE:
It is the uncommon that makes commonplace structures—in this case, the walls—focal points of delight. Faux-painted grass-cloth walls by LR Designs add lovely texture and tone. No bedroom is complete without luxurious custom bedding (Mask Designs). The room is brought together with a cashmere throw, shredded leather accent pillows, a hair-on-hide area rug and a captivating African mask.
Photograph by Gerald Ringgold

FACING PAGE:
The rich opulence of this kitchen has been achieved with custom cherry-glazed cabinetry (K&H Cabinets), porcelain tile (Best Tile) and granite tops. Uncommon touches such as Venetian plastered walls (Rhythmic Walls) and a tin ceiling add unique eye-catching interest. Contractor: Goldsborough Design Build.
Photograph by Gerald Ringgold

LR DESIGNS
Lorra Rivers
130 R Street Northeast
Washington, D.C. 20002
202.526.4580
f: 202.526.4581
www.lrdesignsonline.com

Pamela Gaylin **Ryder**

PAMELA GAYLIN RYDER, INC.

Pamela Gaylin Ryder's love of antiques and timeless, comfortable interiors and a commitment to quality materials grew out of her 10-year stint as manager of Washington's La Provence de Pierre Deux. With degrees in interior design and business from Mount Vernon College, she launched her own firm in 1990, working initially with many of her first clients from this retail design experience. Today, the native Californian's projects range from stately Georgetown mansions to New England seaside homes and Caribbean escapes.

While Pamela emphasizes the importance of pursuing the best quality one can afford, encouraging clients to wait until they can afford the few pieces that will distinguish their environment, her firm is also adept at working with accessories and fabrics that pull a project together and create distinctive livable interiors. She possesses a talent for combining the everyday and the special together into beautiful rooms. A sofa dressed in sailcloth, for example, accentuated with pillows in a luxurious fabric, can achieve the beautiful look that clients seek.

Pamela's interiors, which have been featured in such publications as *Architectural Digest, House Beautiful, Town & Country* and *Traditional Home,* and in such Washington area showhouses as the National Symphony Orchestra Decorators'

Showhouse and the Alexandria Showhouse, are most often described as radiating warmth. She favors a sophisticated look with an emphasis on classic design. She likes to include antiques or furniture with a patina to anchor a room and give visual emphasis. The judicious use of rich patterned fabrics and luxurious materials—embroidered pillows combined with a cashmere throw, for example—add texture and pattern, especially in new homes with bigger footprints.

ABOVE:
The foyer was designed to represent an old sea captain's home. Austrian wide flooring and a painted compass rose work well in the crossroads of this house.
Photograph by Gordon Beall

FACING PAGE:
The family room opens to the kitchen with a spectacular view of the ocean. The fireplace surround was inspired by 18th-century delft tiles.
Photograph by Gordon Beall

Pamela delivers creative solutions that address desires while she stresses the importance of helping clients realize the limitations of their space as well as its possibilities. A dream of a Tuscan kitchen without the requisite space can be satisfied by cabinets painted in the regional palette to introduce a key element of the mood of the beloved style.

Pamela, who is now working on a cottage at a private club in the Caribbean, is adept at handling specialized projects. Working in diverse geographic locales has given her experience handling variances in light, packing containers for international shipment, and specifying individualized environment-appropriate fabrics, hardware and color palettes. "It's about knowing how fabrics will look in the actual light," says Pamela, "what colors work in any given location, and how the particular climate will affect materials."

TOP LEFT:
In the dining room soft colors of blue and white are combined with a custom iron chandelier that was designed to avoid obstructing an ocean view.
Photograph by Gordon Beall

BOTTOM LEFT:
Warm woods in French and English-style furniture are used in the breakfast room where there is a fantastic view to watch the boats and sea life.
Photograph by Gordon Beall

FACING PAGE TOP:
A relaxing atmosphere in the master bedroom was created with the detail of a barrel-vaulted ceiling and soft shades of blue and white.
Photograph by Gordon Beall

FACING PAGE BOTTOM:
Soothing shades of blue and white were used in the living room to showcase the client's extensive art collection.
Photograph by Gordon Beall

Q&A

More about Pamela ...

WHAT PERSONAL INDULGENCE DO YOU SPEND THE MOST MONEY ON?
Travel and luxury items.

WHAT COLOR BEST DESCRIBES YOU?
Greens, all shades with a shot of accent color, like coral.

IF YOU COULD ELIMINATE ONE STYLE FROM THE WORLD WHAT WOULD IT BE?
Mission style.

PAMELA GAYLIN RYDER, INC.
Pamela Gaylin Ryder
5208 MacArthur Boulevard Northwest
Washington, D.C. 20016
202.686.1086
f: 202.686.9737
www.pamelagaylinryder.com

José **Solís**
Paul **Sherrill**

SOLIS BETANCOURT

José Solís, founder and president of Solis Betancourt Inc., has had a lifelong infatuation with art and architecture. Growing up in San Juan, Puerto Rico, he dedicated his spare time during his preparatory years to drawing and painting, which provided him with great communication skills that would come in handy as he professionally trained as an architect at Cornell University. He later gained years of experience at Skidmore, Owings & Merrill and honed his interior design expertise working with John Saladino in New York City.

Three years after founding Solis Betancourt Inc. in 1989, José took Paul Sherrill under his wing, and he was eventually named partner and now serves as the vice president of the company. Paul, a native of North Carolina, was greatly influenced by his grandparents who were painters and weavers. These influences led him to study art and design throughout his childhood. Having received numerous scholarships and attending The Patterson Preparatory School, he further concentrated on his artistic studies. He then trained and graduated with Honors from the University of North Carolina at Greensboro with a Bachelor of Science degree in Human and Environmental Sciences and a degree in art. In 1992, he relocated to Washington, D.C. and began working as an interior designer for

Solis Betancourt, Inc. "José Solis Betancourt has certainly been my most influential mentor and someone that I constantly admire for his enormous creativity and his determination and dedication to fully exploring the design process," he remarked about Solis. Paul soon flourished at Solís Betancourt and he further developed the business to include custom designed furnishings and lighting.

With an international client roster, Solis Betancourt has accepted numerous award-winning commissions and has created a signature collection of lighting in collaboration with Holly Hunt Showrooms. For José and Paul, their ultimate goal is the appropriate individualization of each project. Following an academic approach to integrating architecture and interiors while striving to achieve function and

ABOVE:
Subtle details are executed within a neutral envelope to add visual interest without overpowering the collector's objects of art.
Photograph by Gordon Beall

FACING PAGE:
Playful wooden sculptures of spheres are placed above a somber but grand-scaled mantle, which becomes the backdrop for the casual seating area.
Photograph by Gordon Beall

comfort, Solis Betancourt's designs maintain proportion and harmony. Both José and Paul believe that symmetry and balance are fundamental elements of design that must be acknowledged to create harmonious spaces; addressing the power of axial relationships helps to understandably organize spaces and creates a proper hierarchy.

With skills well grounded in the classical orders, the company has developed substantial experience with contemporary design. In order to further their ability to meet each client's requirements, the firm has developed close working relationships with national and international consultants and contractors in various fields such as lighting, textiles, antiques, contemporary furnishings, millwork, metallurgy and conservations of all types. Through repeated work with this select group, Solis Betancourt can better assure delivery of the design solution.

While their client base is quite diverse and they prefer a wide range of design styles, many of José and Paul's clients have numerous homes in different areas of the world, so this variety is important. The pair enjoys the opportunity to collaborate with other talented and creative professionals in an environment where everyone can share and learn from one another. "When everyone is on the same page of creating an excellent and exciting new product, it is much easier to achieve a brilliant space. This synergy can only happen when egos are left at the door and the room is filled with mutual respect for one another," noted Paul.

Solis Betancourt's projects have been regularly featured in national and international shelter magazines such as *Architectural Digest, House & Garden, House Beautiful, Southern Accents, The New York Times Magazine* and *The Washington Post Magazine.*

ABOVE:
Yards of velvet fabric soften this dramatically vaulted entry foyer leading to the sculptural cantilevered stairway.
Photograph by Gordon Beall

FACING PAGE:
A complex and graphic Oscar Soles painting in acrylic becomes the focal point when entering this intimate seating area of a private library.
Photograph by Gordon Beall

ABOVE:
Electronically operated suede draperies provide privacy and darkness when needed, without obstructing the beautiful gallery of windows to the treehouse view.
Photograph by Gordon Beall

FACING PAGE TOP:
A romantic French Aubusson tapestry adds perspective and depth to this windowless wall.
Photograph by Gordon Beall

FACING PAGE BOTTOM:
Tobacco leaf wall covering and rough plank cabinetry are paired with sumptuous velvet upholstery to create a warm and richly textured palette.
Photograph by Gordon Beall

Q&A

More about José & Paul ...

IF YOU COULD ELIMINATE ONE DESIGN/ARCHITECTURAL/BUILDING TECHNIQUE OR STYLE FROM THE WORLD, WHAT WOULD IT BE?
Objections to historical styles of design in the contemporary abstract are a bit unfair. We have learned and can greatly learn from all design and study its relevance by understanding the climate in which it was created.

WHAT IS THE HIGHEST COMPLIMENT YOU'VE RECEIVED PROFESSIONALLY?
It is always rewarding to have a client acknowledge that our work has had a positive change to their lives; but the best compliment was when a client said that our work had brought a whole new inner peace to their lives.

WHAT IS THE BEST PART OF BEING AN INTERIOR DESIGNER?
We believe that spirituality can and does exist in art and that interior design is a form of three-dimensional art. Therefore, creating spaces that can positively influence the inhabitants is truly rewarding.

HOW CAN WE TELL THAT YOU LIVE IN THIS LOCALE?
Washington, D.C. has the intellectual and cultural benefits of a large urban city and the ease and comfort of a town.

WHAT EXCITES YOU MOST ABOUT BEING PART OF *SPECTACULAR HOMES*?
The Washington, Potomac and Chesapeake area has gone unnoticed as a place for great design and is overshadowed by other industries such as government. However, there is an incredible talent that exists here and a relaxed style that is an amalgamation of our nation's own diverse styles mixed with a dose of Southern influence while acknowledging the affluence of the international community.

SOLIS BETANCOURT
José Solís
Paul Sherrill
1739 Connecticut Avenue
Washington, D.C. 20009
202.659.8734
www.solisbetancourt.com

Andy Staszak

ANDY STASZAK INTERIOR DESIGN

When Andy Staszak was 19 years old, one of his aunts hired an interior designer and an art consultant. Privy to every aspect of this project, the experience left Andy forever impressed by the power of design to create rich and gratifying environments, spaces which reflect the occupants' personalities and satisfy their everyday needs.

His basic approach to design is rooted in tradition but tempered by a strong infusion of modern elements. Whichever style he chooses for a given project, his fondness for warm colors and furniture with clean lines prevails. And he firmly believes that all objects need not produce the same visual impact. "One doesn't need to love everything in a room," he muses. "If everything is so individual, your eye doesn't know where to focus because pieces compete for the viewer's attention and unique and interesting objects become lost."

In short, he tends to juxtapose strong graphic elements with more passive elements, providing settings within which objects stand out sharply. For example, he might center a strongly-contoured black coffee table atop a pale rug. Or, a curvilinear French armchair might be silhouetted against a table covered in an unadorned woven cloth.

What especially excites Andy is finding the perfect balance between his clients' practical needs and their stylistic preferences. How do they spend their days? Do they entertain frequently? Do they require plenty of seating because they invite lots of friends over to watch TV? Do they serve meals buffet-style or at sit-down dinners? Do their quarters need freshening up? More punch? A bit of sexiness? Taking these considerations into account, Andy integrates them into a sound design framework which determines the choice and arrangement of furniture and objects, color scheme, lighting plan, etc., each playing its characteristic role.

Andy strives to achieve balance in a space by bringing areas of greater and lesser weight into a state of equilibrium. For instance, he might include big pieces of art which provide visual weight but do not occupy valuable floor space. He also realizes that the rich heritage of antiques adds weight, thus increasing the stature of a room and altering its tone.

ABOVE:
Bronze walls that were air brushed with nine layers of glaze add to the overall warmth of this room.
Photograph by Gwin Hunt

FACING PAGE:
An elegant coffee table and an Asian antique console anchor a room with neutral-colored upholstery in a variety of textures.
Photograph by Gwin Hunt

Andy's color palettes exude warmth and body as they interact with light to produce various expressive effects. He pays close attention to how color adjusts to ambient light as it changes throughout the day, culminating in the drama of nighttime lighting. Orchestrated pinpoint halogen recessed lighting systems on multiple circuits combine with lamps to provide both shafts and pools of interweaving light from many levels.

Window treatments amplify the qualities of light and color. For a client who entertains with afternoon teas for fundraising events, Andy contrived to assure that the room was at its best at four in the afternoon. He used sheer wool (one of his favorite window textiles) to fashion soft Roman shades. The fabric, in concert with the late afternoon sun, provides a beautiful golden glow to the room. At night the shades create a scrim which eliminates the forbidding look of black window glass, infusing the space with warmth—both visually and psychologically.

Successfully rearranging the possessions his clients already have and wish to continue to use reveals one of Andy's greatest talents. He views the process as a mathematical equation—these are the unchangeable "givens"—the challenge becomes finding a solution that will incorporate the old with the new. For example, in one four-bedroom house, with living room, dining room, family room, and study, Andy added only four pieces of furniture—a coffee table and lounge chair in the family room, a dining room table, and an antique Chinese altar table which

unified the previously isolated end walls of the living room. Along with the judicious rearrangement of furniture and objects, reframing and re-hanging of pictures, fresh color in fabric and paint and new lighting, the whole impression of the house was completely transformed, surprising and delighting its owners, whose reactions to their home had always been lukewarm. It is, as a matter of fact, the response of Andy Staszak's clients which gives him the greatest pleasure from his work. He is content when, after the completion of a house, his clients beam with enthusiasm, happily telling him how much they love entertaining and just living in their home.

ABOVE LEFT:
This neutral color palette was punched up a notch with the use of accessories, including coral-colored lamps and a stunning piece of art.
Photograph by Gwin Hunt

ABOVE RIGHT:
An unusual chandelier and custom-made furniture make this room an elegant and sophisticated space to dine.
Photograph by Gwin Hunt

FACING PAGE TOP:
By using balance instead of symmetry, a warm and casual feel is introduced to this formal living room.
Photograph by Gwin Hunt

FACING PAGE BOTTOM:
The graphic nature of the dark wood side table has a sculptural feel in this contemporary room.
Photograph by Gwin Hunt

ANDY STASZAK INTERIOR DESIGN
Andy Staszak
1521 Wisconsin Avenue Northwest, #3
Washington, D.C. 20007
202.337.3345

DESIGNER: Frederike Hecht, Frederike's Designs, *Page 123*

DESIGNER: Arlene Critzos, Interior Concepts, Inc., *Page 107*

DESIGNER: Kelley Proxmire, Kelley Interior Design Service, *Page 147*

Maryland

Sue Burgess
BURGESS INTERIORS

Although Sue Burgess says she doesn't have rules when it comes to conceiving her designs, she displays exceptional congruity and a savvy for spotting tomorrow's classics. Her work has been featured twice on the cover of *House Beautiful* as well as in *Southern Accents, Traditional Home* and *Beautiful Southern Homes*, all accomplishments that speak to the caliber of her work and ability to understand the context of a space in the broadest sense.

Sue has been a designer for 35 years and has owned her design business for the last 20 years in Maryland where she has lived since attending college. A self-professed "small operation," the size of her business certainly does not reflect the size of her ideas or experience! "I make sure that every home lives up to its full potential," says Burgess, who precisely plots space arrangements, making sure the overall scale and proportion are well balanced.

She also admits to two weaknesses, Paris and symmetry, which in the design world aren't attributes so much as the perfect set of qualifications. Her style is a classic, simple approach with ageless elements shaping a consistently livable, easy-to-mix style. Sue's signature palette of off whites accented with natural greens and browns gives a flawless balance between opacity and translucence. With lines that are consistently clean, sophisticated yet casually minded, architectural details are carefully crafted to draw character from every aspect of the design.

In Sue's interiors, enhancing a space while incorporating treasured possessions is a must. You'll find a spare but layered mix of inherited antiques and custom pieces amid Paris flea market prizes. But, the design must also suit the intended purpose of the room, and Sue makes sure to focus on the interpreted needs and particular style of each client. To their delight, she lends a comfortable approach to cosmopolitan style, bringing together fresh, pleasing spaces perfectly appropriate to everyday living.

ABOVE:
Master bedroom with custom mirror and bench by Burgess Interiors.
Photograph by Gordon Beall

FACING PAGE:
Living room with antique Biedermeier secretary and antique Lyre-back bench.
Photograph by Gordon Beall

ABOVE:
Living room with mirror-backed antique bronze grill and custom Klismos chair.
Photograph by Gordon Beall

FACING PAGE:
Office at Burgess Interiors with custom console, antique settee from Paris flea market and framed intaglios.
Photograph by Gordon Beall

More about Sue ...

WHAT SIZE IS YOUR COMPANY?
It's small but very hands on! Just myself, a part-time assistant and a bookkeeper.

HOW LONG HAVE YOU LIVED IN THE D.C. AREA?
A long time! I've lived in the Washington, D.C. area since attending Mount Vernon College.

IF YOU COULD ELIMINATE ONE ARCHITECTURAL STYLE FROM THE WORLD, WHAT WOULD IT BE?
I don't like bad additions or renovations to existing homes. When the overall scale and architectural details aren't in keeping with the rest of the house, it's too abrupt and difficult to ignore the obvious interruption in the cohesion.

WHAT ELEMENT OF STYLE OR PHILOSOPHY HAVE YOU STUCK WITH OVER THE YEARS THAT STILL WORKS FOR YOU TODAY?
Simple design without all the excess; I can be comfortable with blank spaces until the perfect element is found.

BURGESS INTERIORS
Sue Burgess
4411 Bradley Lane
Chevy Chase, MD 20815
301.652.6217
c: 301.775.1150

ABOVE TOP:
Entry hall with faux striped floor.
Photograph by Gordon Beall

ABOVE BOTTOM:
Dining room Dutch portrait with custom dining chairs by Burgess Interiors.
Photograph by Gordon Beall

FACING PAGE:
Kitchen with oak and mahogany antique Barley Twist console.
Photograph by Gordon Beall

Alex Clymer

ALEX CLYMER INTERIORS, LTD.

Alex Clymer doesn't work like most other designers; she finds unique solutions for her clients' design dreams, even if that means spending months to find a piece that is an exact fit in the design scheme of a room. Principal and head designer of her firm, Alex Clymer Interiors, Ltd., Alex strives to ensure ACI's creation of comfortable, luxurious, livable interiors that reflect each client's needs and personal lifestyle. The secret to Alex's great success lies in the careful attention to details and her sense of style, accompanied by over 20 years of experience and education. Much of her highly acclaimed work has been inspired by the people and places she has come across in her work and travels as well as the ongoing search for interesting objects and the use of new, exciting resources.

A firm believer of the concept that a person's home is their haven, Alex interweaves a harmonious environment in all her homes as part of the total design concept. In an effort to ensure her clients' awareness of their senses and the needs and feeling those senses arouse, Alex designs rooms which promote a feeling of well-being and tranquility. "We need to know how to infuse our surroundings with colors that please and textures that add interest when a monochromatic setting is called for. Our life spaces should be able to reenergize us and foster creativity. They should bring us pleasure and enable us to be ourselves, or who we aspire to be."

LEFT:
Found character; a soft water-colored palette of glazed walls and a washed Venetian plaster stenciled ceiling add dimension to a room void of architectural elements.
Photograph by Alan Gilbert

Alex keeps her clients involved throughout the project and develops solutions for their spaces that are specifically tailored for them.

ACI offers full design services, including pre-construction, new construction and reconstruction consultation. Always insistent upon a strong collaboration between client and designer, Alex works with each new client to develop successful and meaningful designs for one room or an entire home. Commitment to high-quality service and accessibility to clients is a mission she embarks upon with each project.

ABOVE:
Quiet drama; a beautiful blending of soft tones and varied textures creates a dining room that enhances the senses and encourages one to stay.
Photograph by Alan Gilbert

FACING PAGE TOP:
Glittering tablescape; mixture of china, crystal and sterling flatware affords one the luxury of indulgence with their moods and styles.
Photograph by Alan Gilbert

FACING PAGE BOTTOM:
Sensuous seclusion; this luxurious 2,000-square-foot master bedroom retreat exudes comfort and elegance. Fabric wall allows optimal placement of bed for the magnificent river view.
Photograph by Keel Harris

As a certified designer and past president of the Maryland Chapter of the American Society of Interior Designers, Alex has been featured in various national and local publications and works from coast to coast. Her projects are as diverse as she is and include the Delegate's Lounge in Maryland's State House, a multiple suite at M&T Bank Stadium, a workout center for women, yachts and primary and secondary residences.

Alex spends a great amount of time familiarizing herself with clients' personalities and ideas in order to provide them with an endless list of ideas and options. Staying as far away as possible from cookie-cutter type designs, she communicates with each client to find the perfect solution in order to make them happy and meet their expectations, no matter how high they might be. ACI stresses that good design is about the original and not the copy and invites clients new and old to eagerly discover the possibilities of a new project with their design consultation.

TOP LEFT:
Enhanced glow; a soft metallic ceiling washes this monochromatic room with Old World charm, while a Tobiasse painting offers a punch of color and an intriguing mix.
Photograph by Gwin Hunt

BOTTOM LEFT:
Dramatic entrance; this open two-story foyer is adorned with a custom Venetian plaster ceiling washed in soft silver and golds. The black wall provides the perfect backdrop for an art collection.
Photograph by Gwin Hunt

FACING PAGE TOP:
Timeless jewel; this music room invites one to linger. Ethereal ceiling murals tell a story while the custom designed moulding with antique mirror echoes the color and light.
Photograph by John Coyle

FACING PAGE BOTTOM:
A touch of theatre; this whimsical powder room with its full-size jester and delightfully quirky monkey adds a touch of the unexpected.
Photograph by Gwin Hunt

Q & A

More about Alex ...

WHAT IS THE BEST PART OF BEING AN INTERIOR DESIGNER?
I thoroughly enjoy the diversity I experience in each project and the opportunity to create environments that people enjoy living in.

WHAT IS THE HIGHEST COMPLIMENT YOU'VE RECEIVED PROFESSIONALLY?
Kudos and awards are always special, but when our clientele evoke genuine emotions of pleasure and joy, this by far is the greatest compliment.

WHAT ONE ELEMENT OF STYLE HAVE YOU STUCK WITH FOR YEARS THAT STILL WORKS FOR YOU TODAY?
I try not to have a signature look. The finished project is about my client and not ACI. We always start off with a basic palette and weave our various elements of styles from there; balance and proportion are intricate parts of our design.

IF YOU COULD ELIMINATE ONE DESIGN TECHNIQUE OR STYLE FROM THE WORLD WHAT WOULD IT BE?
Television shows and shelter magazines that make every person think they're a "decorator." While they have their place, your home should evolve and not be an instant makeover or someone else's signature.

ALEX CLYMER INTERIORS, LTD.
Alex Clymer, CID, ASID
86 Maryland Avenue
Annapolis, MD 21401
410.263.0992
f: 410.263.4895
www.alexclymerinteriors.com

Arlene **Critzos**

INTERIOR CONCEPTS, INC.

Founder and President of Interior Concepts, Inc., Arlene Critzos is an award-winning, well-known interior designer who heads ICI as a full-service firm specializing in high-end residential and commercial interiors and a division of award-winning model home design. Arlene takes great pride and pleasure in creating what she believes is the most valuable facet of a person's life—their environment. "I love having the opportunity to affect people from the moment they walk in their home; it is their haven."

Developing her creative design and professional expertise combined with the clients' wish lists, Arlene produces truly successful, personalized interiors. Arlene's unique, breathtaking designs are often inspired, if not at least contributed to, by her years of global travel. After studying in places such as Rome, Holland and the U.K. and working in Mainland China, Jordan, Spain and more, she developed a comfortable appeal for international interiors and a personal style she calls "European Traditional."

Although she has traveled around the world and back, Arlene is happy to call Annapolis home. She finds the town to be a small-town sanctuary which draws many people from faraway places to settle permanently. "They have come here to

nest and we are chosen, in many cases, to create their living habitats. It is a town that is open to good design," said Arlene.

Arlene works on an assortment of projects ranging from large architectural projects to smaller room-based projects. She begins the projects with the architecture—moving walls, creating ceilings, designing the furnishings and finishes; then the accessorizing is the final and very important phase.

Interior Concepts has designed major spaces in the Middle East, China, England and Spain and in various U.S. states.

ABOVE:
A series of geometric quads create this perfect loggia which connects all the rooms on the main level. Accented mouldings in custom plaster and medallions finish each area. Furnished as a gallery of art, boulle furniture and antique accent chairs complete the space. The floor is crafted of stone and wood.
Photograph by Gordon Beall

FACING PAGE:
The designer strategically positioned the living room in the center of the house to make sure that it was used. Twenty-four-foot ceilings with two-story gothic windows create the architecture. A powerful classical painting of monk and child from the school of Murillo fills the space. Three seating areas complement each other all in various neutral tones and textures. Occasional pieces mix wood, stone, metal and antique washed Venetian woods.
Photograph by Gordon Beall

ABOVE:
This billiard room has multiple areas and functions. Seating at an antique English walnut fireplace, billiard area, music area and a game table complete this space. A 19th-century, 12-foot silver leaded French doorway sets the stage as you enter the room. A palate of reds, ochre, olive, chocolate and black warms this space. A mix of sisal, Orientals and animal prints layer as "floor cloths." The red center sofa is the anchor for all other patterns. Leather, tapestries and antique textiles complement each other. The high ceiling is beamed while large plaster gothic plaques fill the slopes of the ceiling.
Photograph by Gordon Beall

Q&A

More about Arlene ...

WHAT PERSONAL INDULGENCE DO YOU SPEND THE MOST MONEY ON?
My two passions: horses and travel.

WHAT COLOR BEST DESCRIBES YOU AND WHY?
Taupe for its great neutrality and red for its bold pop. I love the versatile nature of neutrals because I can punctuate them with art and color.

YOU CAN TELL I LIVE IN THIS LOCALE BECAUSE I ...
Well, you can't! I have lived in and studied many places throughout the world, so my work really has a global reference. That does not mean I do not love this locale, though. I love the proximity of the ocean and the nostalgia of the downtown areas, all within close proximity to one of the country's greatest cities, Washington, D.C. Many interiors here in Annapolis are casual and coastal, but there is always room for a little reference to the arts.

NAME ONE THING PEOPLE DON'T KNOW ABOUT YOU.
I am an open book, a very straightforward personality. I have a passion for vegetable gardening and cooking.

WHAT IS THE BEST PART OF BEING AN INTERIOR DESIGNER?
I truly enjoy the endlesss creative path, the continual growth of knowledge and interacting with the client to a great end result.

WHO HAS HAD THE BIGGEST INFLUENCE ON YOUR CAREER?
My parents were supportive of me from the inception of my career. They saw no boundaries for me and gave me a life of various ethnic influences.

INTERIOR CONCEPTS, INC.
Arlene Critzos
2560 Riva Road
Annapolis, MD 21401
410.224.7366
f: 301.970.8013
www.interiorconceptsinc.com

ABOVE TOP:
An outdoor haven with water views, this photo captures an interior wall with an over-scaled marble side table, great for outdoor buffets. Above it is an antique architectural turn-of-the-century metal window frame from France hung as art and embraced by two iron sconces. Multiple seating areas join this table in the room's composition.
Photograph by Gordon Beall

ABOVE BOTTOM:
A great transition area to the porch, outdoor fireplace and eating area, the fresco-style painted stallions set the theme art for the outdoors. Taken from a historic "plaz" in Salzburg, Austria, these horses provided design inspiration. Arched openings draped in sheer gauze add movement and warmth. A handmade twig chair and ottoman remain outdoors all year.
Photograph by Gordon Beall

Ronald Craig **Godshalk**

RONALD CRAIG GODSHALK INTERIOR

Ronald Craig Godshalk has always known he wanted to be a designer. Coming from a family of artists, he enjoyed a freedom from convention that allowed his creativity to flourish. As a small child, he would rearrange his mother's furniture, playing with the sense of space, though at the time he thought he was simply playing! As a student at the National Art Academy, he used part of his tuition to buy a late 18th-century grandfather clock made in Scotland by John Allen. His father was furious until a clockmaker friend recognized the piece's fineness. Ronald was forgiven and his passion for collecting art and antiques was established.

While Ronald's projects, which include his work for such showhouses as the Southern Maryland Decorator Showhouse, reflect his lifelong passion for antiques, his architectural training allows for the confident blending of different periods. Walls, floors, window treatments and millwork are everything in creating a beautiful interior. He emphasizes setting the stage so that furnishings can be incidental.

Approaching the design process with integrity and balancing creativity with programmatic detail, Ronald defines his clients' desires as well as their needs and helps them to articulate their unique sensibilities.

LEFT:
This historic Antebellum home, built in 1850, is located in Charles County, Maryland and is the designer's personal residence. In keeping with the home's authenticity and as a beautiful setting to display his love of antiques and art, the designer featured gold tones in these sitting and dining rooms. On the dining table, part of a vast collection, are antique Chinese Canton blue and white porcelain vases.
Photograph by Kenneth Wyner

Meetings in the clients' home, spending hours talking about their lifestyles and intimately getting to know who they are is as important as knowing how a space will be put to use. Many times, Ronald's keen eye deciphers non-verbal clues, giving him valuable insight that might otherwise go unnoticed. He can tell toward what design direction they lean simply by their clothes or, even, the color of their car. And, with clients from across the country, Ronald is well versed in every dialect, picking up the tiniest of clues and cleverly spinning them into vision and reality.

Establishing a conceptual direction, Ronald likes to sleep on his designs and tries to dream about them. "That probably sounds a bit feigned, but it's absolutely true," says Godshalk, "but many, many of my ideas do come to me in the middle of the night!" Never drawing his ideas from books or magazines, Ronald refines each design with balance and proportion. Color, an important element of each plan, is expertly evened throughout, and ingeniously offset furnishings placed by weight and size lend a flow that calms while drawing the eye around the room. Eclectic and elegant, Ronald never loses sight of the architecture that sets the framework. The results are completely original environments that refuse to be typecast by a particular period or style and are a visual communication of his clients' every wish.

Though Ronald is able to progress readily through a myriad of different styles, his personal taste is traditional yet transitional, a sanguine combination of different periods contiguously mingling modern and old. Though the feeling may be haphazard, his placement is intentional with classic proportions featured prominently in each room. Having blurred the boundaries between art and design, Ronald challenges assumptions and lets his interiors tell a story of plucked motifs and custom palettes. Fresh, pleasing environments that defy precedent and transcend boundaries are undoubtedly the hallmark of Ronald's sought-after designs.

ABOVE:
At first glance, the most interesting element of this room is the suspended hand-carved antique angels. However, one should know that this morning room was an addition built expressly around the chandelier. The expansive size of it did not allow entrance through door or window, so the room was quite literally built around it with careful attention to the corresponding design scale of the room.
Photograph by Kenneth Wyner

FACING PAGE:
This master bedroom, in striking reds, boasts a plethora of interesting antiques. The left corner of the room houses an 18th-century Beau Brummell soldier's chest meant to store personal items during wartime. Over the fireplace hangs an important painting by Bogert.
Photograph by Kenneth Wyner

Q&A

More about Ronald...

WHAT DO YOU FEEL IS THE MOST IMPORTANT ELEMENT OF DESIGN?
Color ... I am tired of 42 shades of beige!

WHAT IS YOUR FAVORITE PIECE IN YOUR OWN HOME?
A 10½-foot-tall French case clock.

ON WHAT PROJECTS ARE YOU CURRENTLY WORKING?
I am working on two homes in Virginia and one in Maryland. They are very large, historic, landmark homes that have been ongoing projects for about three years. I've done lots of custom pieces, such as 11-foot Chippendale sofas, mixed with heirloom antiques.

WHAT WOULD BE YOUR IDEAL PROJECT?
Anything that is ground up! I don't get to do them very often, but I have a couple of clients with whom I've done a number of homes. I have picked out the grounds and the architect, staked out how the house was to be situated on the ground taking full advantage of the gorgeous views ... basically planned everything, making sure that the house functions well. The rest falls right into place!

RONALD CRAIG GODSHALK INTERIOR
Ronald Craig Godshalk
PO Box 12017
Saint Petersburg, FL 33733
301.752.4081
727.368.6463

ABOVE & FACING PAGE:
These two photos offer a different vantage point of the entryway. The magnificent original heart pine flooring has been restored to its original charm. Complementing antiques such as the French tall case clock (circa 1710), Louis XVI chair and butler's desk are carefully on display upon entry.
Photograph by Kenneth Wyner

Diane **Gordy**
DGI DESIGN GROUP

Diane Gordy, CID, ASID, founded DGI Design Group on four basic principles: quality, excellence, loyalty and trust. Striving to exceed her clients' expectations, she keeps their needs in focus, adding value wherever possible. Diane thoroughly immerses her energy into each project and proactively directs her design teams to consistently meet project objectives.

A graduate of the American University and currently enrolled in the School of Architecture and Planning at Catholic University in Washington, D.C., Diane is a lifelong student and never passes up the opportunity to learn. Not one to follow trends in her life, she also avoids them in her work. "Good design is timeless. I follow no fads. Often when I return from buying trips, new clients may ask about the latest styles I've seen and I say, 'I didn't really notice any!' It's true! If you think about it, what does 'new' mean? I constantly experiment and innovate ways to use materials and work very hard to stay current with the latest technological developments and applications related to Zero-energy design, but, as a designer of the built environment, I never focus on fleeting fancies and encourage my clients to get out of the mainstream. They need to develop their own style. They may not know what that is, but together we can find it." Her lifelong philosophy

has been to never impose her style or personal design preferences on her clients. Rather, she consistently conveys a certain intensity that relates to the senses of the human body by creating works that stir excitement and create an emotional response, all within an envelope that answers the problems of the program with an environmental sensitivity.

ABOVE:
An English Regency-style parlor provides a retreat for reading and quiet conversation.
Photograph by Celia Pearson

FACING PAGE:
An Oushak carpet grounds rattan pieces from the Far East and English bench-made elements in this cheerful sunroom.
Photograph by Celia Pearson

Diane is also a trusted team leader when executing the complex interior design process and applies analytical problem-solving skills and acute intuitive intelligence to all of her projects. "You have to anticipate and prepare for the completely unexpected in this 'Murphy's Law' kind of business. Thinking on your feet and quickly solving problems to achieve the design intent is every bit as important as having the most brilliant design intent imaginable. Knowing how to mediate and when to 'go along to get along' is also important."

Diane's extensive design career has spanned over 25 years, but she still remembers the defining moment in which she realized her career was the culmination of her dreams. "This happened over 20 years ago. I was hired by someone who had inherited a fabulous cache of 18th-century American antiques. While taking photographs and dimensioning the pieces, I recognized a highboy and lowboy made by a famous Philadelphia cabinetmaker. I remember going home that evening and rapturously telling my husband that should I die in my sleep that very night, he needed to know that I was professionally satisfied by having had this opportunity to work with antiques of the stature I had studied in school. It was an electrifying experience."

The combination of Diane's dedication to continuing education, her commitment to excellence and extensive practical experience as well as her complete accessibility means her clients return to her time and time again. As the coordinator of services, both her clients and their contractors know she is only a cell phone call or an e-mail message away and can be reached at any time to settle the things that require quick changes or adjustments to achieve the expected design intent within unexpected constraints.

ABOVE:
Repetitive use of strong geometric shapes grounds the irrational and asymmetrical volumes of this dynamic contemporary space.
Photograph by Lisa Masson

FACING PAGE TOP:
Finishing off the attic of the Victorian beachhouse gives these owners a spectacular view of the Atlantic Ocean.
Photograph by Celia Pearson

FACING PAGE BOTTOM:
Multi-armed chandelier brings the heroic ceiling height down to human scale.
Photograph by Ron Solomon

Q&A

More about Diane ...

WHAT PERSONAL INDULGENCES DO YOU SPEND THE MOST MONEY ON?
Education and travel. I have traveled and studied extensively, at home and abroad. Wherever I go, I fill sketchbooks with vignettes and details of intriguing examples of architecture and interior design.

WHAT IS THE HIGHEST COMPLIMENT YOU'VE RECEIVED PROFESSIONALLY?
My clients often tell me after many years of living and/or working in an environment I've designed that they still love their spaces as much as when they were first completed.

WHAT IS THE SINGLE THING YOU WOULD DO TO BRING A DULL HOUSE TO LIFE?
Add light, either from an additional light source or with reflective materials like cut crystal.

WHO HAS HAD THE BIGGEST INFLUENCE ON YOUR CAREER?
My husband. For instance, one night, I was up late designing townhouses for a small development he and I are doing together in Florida. I printed out the design and left it for him at the breakfast table. His comment was, "I've always so enjoyed your ingenuity." I bask in the warmth of his praise, even after all these years!

HAVE YOU RECEIVED ANY AWARDS OR SPECIAL RECOGNITION?
I've won national recognition from the American Wood Council and have served on the ASID National International Legislative Advisory Council and the Washington Metro Chapter ASID Government and Public Affairs Team, winning Presidential citations for leadership. I am currently on the Maryland State Board of Certified Interior Designers and am working on an interior design education initiative for the state.

DGI DESIGN GROUP
Diane Gordy, CID, ASID
7307 MacArthur Boulevard, Suite 214
Bethesda, MD 20816
301.229.9500
www.dgidesigngroup.com

John **Hale**
Joy **Rexroad**

HALE & REXROAD INTERIOR DESIGN

As design partners for more than 25 years, John Hale and Joy Rexroad bring together their unique perspectives to create a design approach that maximizes their considerable talents while still reflecting the desires and budget of the client. Based in Baltimore, John and Joy work primarily in residential settings from Vermont to Florida. Their interiors have been featured in Baltimore Symphony Decorators' Showhouses for more than 20 years and showcased in such publications as *House Beautiful, Style, Traditional Home* and *The Baltimore Sun.*

John holds a degree in accounting from the University of Baltimore and a degree in interior design from the Maryland Institute, College of Art. Joy studied design at the University of Maryland, and earned a degree from the Maryland Institute, College of Art. John and Joy met in 1975, when Joy began working for a firm owned by John and several partners. When the partners retired, he and Joy formed Hale and Rexroad Interior Design in 1984.

John and Joy are activists for improving and promoting the interior design profession. Both are Maryland State Certified Interior Designers and are active in the Maryland Chapter of American Society of Interior Designers (ASID). John served on the chapter's Board of Directors for more than four years and was President in 2003-2004. Joy has worked on several chapter committees, including the Nominating Committee, and is currently President Elect. John and Joy have co-chaired the chapter's Design Competition for many years. John established an Educational Fund at the chapter that provides money for scholarships and other educational programs.

ABOVE:
This parlor was transformed into an extraordinary room using formal elements that provide both guests and family an opportunity to experience entertaining in a genuine English manor.
Photograph by William Leddon

FACING PAGE:
This reception room uses sheer, white and gold fabrics and finishes along with several French accents to convey a light and airy simplicity that beckons you to come in and make yourself comfortable.
Photograph by Anne Gummerson

HALE & REXROAD INTERIOR DESIGN
John Hale
Joy Rexroad, ASID
200 West Lafayette Avenue
Baltimore, MD 21217
410.669.0410

Photograph by Susan Connolly

Frederike **Hecht**

FREDERIKE'S DESIGNS

F rederike Hecht of Frederike's Designs believes that a designer should transform into a chameleon by finding out what their client loves and making it their own. Frederike's goal in every design project is to create a beautiful, diverse, aesthetically pleasing environment while pleasing her clients and meeting their greatest expectations.

Frederike's Designs, which currently has three employees, has been in the home interior design business for over 18 years. The firm's work has been published in several national and local publications, including *Traditional Home, Better Homes and Gardens, Style, Baltimore Sun* and *County Crier*.

Having established a strong niche as the premier provider of highly customized interior design services in the Mid-Atlantic region, Frederike's Designs' ability to assist homeowners in designing their homes around handpicked design concepts makes them unique in their market. Their customer service and strong relationships with an established group of reputable architects and builders are unparalleled in the industry.

LEFT:
Easy elegance in the kitchen creates a familiar warmth to enjoy any meal. The columns delineate space but encompass the room completely.
Photograph by John J. Coyle Jr./Coyle Commercial Photographics Studios

Priding herself on her level of service and the unique product she offers, Frederike never stops shy of going the extra mile to find the ultimate unique product and make the project a special, meaningful place for her clients. Not only does she design all of the interiors, but she also designs houses and all the miniscule details that go along with them, like floor plans and exterior design. Frederike's greatest satisfaction comes from designing and building houses from scratch. Starting from a piece of paper, she figures out the materials from soup to nuts: every lamp, carpet, fixture, built-in and everything else in between. "The most unique part of my job is that I am very involved with the building and construction. I meet with contractors weekly and spend a lot of time drafting," told the designer.

With most of her projects extremely detailed and over-the-top, it is easy to tell that Frederike's favorite part if the design project is adding her creative touch. It is also easy to tell that she is a naturally gifted designer. "When I chose my profession, I asked myself 'what would I do for free if it was my hobby?' and this is what I chose because it was my natural passion. When you are passionate about something, you do it well. It is not like work; it's fun."

ABOVE LEFT:
Built-in vanity with a gothic palladium window adds character to the master bedroom.
Photograph by John J. Coyle Jr./Coyle Commercial Photographics Studios

ABOVE RIGHT:
This elegant, deep coral-colored dining room has sight lines into the foyer and living room through arches, which creates a fabulous place to dine.
Photograph by John J. Coyle Jr./Coyle Commercial Photographics Studios

FACING PAGE TOP:
A grand entrance invites you into this beautiful home.
Photograph by John J. Coyle Jr./Coyle Commercial Photographics Studios

FACING PAGE BOTTOM:
The kitchen is the family hub. Anyone would enjoy this dramatic mountain lodge kitchen.
Photograph by John J. Coyle Jr./Coyle Commercial Photographics Studios

Q&A

More about Frederike ...

NAME SOMETHING MOST PEOPLE DON'T KNOW ABOUT YOU.
I am fluent in German, a very good tennis player and an avid NFL fan.

WHAT DO YOU LIKE THE MOST ABOUT DOING BUSINESS IN YOUR LOCALE?
Working along the entire Eastern seaboard, I have been involved in many unique and challenging projects encompassing a multitude of different design concepts. I enjoy the diversity of my projects and take great pleasure in creating an environment for my clients that expresses their individuality and makes them feel comfortable and proud of their homes.

WHAT IS THE BEST PART OF BEING AN INTERIOR DECORATOR?
The lifelong friendships that are created with my clients.

YOU WOULDN'T KNOW IT BUT MY FRIENDS WOULD TELL YOU I AM:
Overly generous with my time and affection.

WHAT COLOR BEST DESCRIBES YOU?
Pink, because I have a rosy disposition and am always cheerful.

FREDERIKE'S DESIGNS
Frederike Hecht
12622 Gores Mill Road
Reisterstown, MD 21136
410.526.5882
f: 410.526.1737

Leslie Hunt

LESLIE HUNT INTERIORS

In business since 1975, Leslie Hunt is a designer who is not afraid to try something new. In fact, she got her start in northern Michigan in a time and place where there were no interior designers. "Interior design was the furthest concept from anyone's mind—they all laughed at me," she recalls. Starting right out of college, Leslie took a Victorian house and turned it into a studio showroom, creating a first for her area.

This wouldn't be the only first for Leslie; she continues to work with firsts on a daily basis. In fact, her favorite part of the design process is the first time she sees one of her sketches become a reality. Watching what she has created become a reality is, for Leslie, the height of interior design.

From the time she was a child, Leslie was lucky enough to know that design was her calling. "My family relocated to North Carolina when I was 10 years old, and I was fascinated by the whole design process as we settled into our new home. The interior designer commissioned to do our home worked with me and let me do my whole room. I was hooked from that point on."

Throughout the years, Leslie has become known as "the designer with no ego." Working closely with clients in order to come up with a style unique to them, she focuses on adjusting her tastes to their tastes. She works with many clients who have distinctly different tastes to her own and works through that difference, finding it to be an advantage more than an obstacle.

ABOVE:
The celadon theme is continued in a cozy nook overlooking the Chesapeake Bay.
Photograph by Gwin Hunt

FACING PAGE:
The client's extensive collection of antique celadon porcelain sets the tone for this Annapolis waterfront home.
Photograph by Gwin Hunt

With style in mind, Leslie's objective is to design a home to look like it has been around for years. Using a mixture of pieces so a space appears to be a combination of traditional and contemporary, her spaces most often feel natural and comfortable. It is important to Leslie that the pieces she uses have meaning and a look of importance rather than appearing as though they came straight from the furniture store.

Leslie's goal is for her clients to walk into a room, love everything and feel like it is exactly what they wanted. She will stop at nothing to ensure that goal comes to

fruition and to earn her clients' plaudits. After exhibiting a large variety of selections to her clients and letting them pick and choose, she comes to an understanding of their tastes. Patterns begin to emerge, and body language conveys likes and dislikes. For Leslie, this process is almost intuitive; she can often read a client's facial expressions and body language and immediately know how they feel about an item.

ABOVE:
27-foot ceilings with arches frame this creme and black kitchen in Great Falls, Virginia.
Photograph by Gwin Hunt

FACING PAGE LEFT:
Embroidered silk draperies, trapunto pillows and an antique celadon lamp combine to make an
inviting seating area.
Photograph by Gwin Hunt

FACING PAGE RIGHT:
A Brunschwig & Fils linen picturing many well-loved dog breeds accents this waterfront
dining nook.
Photograph by Gwin Hunt

A very strong art background, including a Bachelor of Fine Arts, has given Leslie the keen ability to understand the building process from inception to finish. Her ability to draw and develop blueprints and put all of her ideas on paper, making them a tangible concept, makes it easier for both clients and the building team to understand the design process. Conveying her ideas through pictures, Leslie ensures that the installer, fabricator and the rest of her design team will be able to make her ideas and her clients' dreams into a reality. With over 20 years of experience working with builders and clients, Leslie ensures that the whole process, from sticks to the finished product, is a work of art.

TOP LEFT:
This Annapolis cottage has one large living area with several distinct functions. The dining area anchors the room.
Photograph by Gwin Hunt

BOTTOM LEFT:
A fireplace seating area forms the central portion of the Annapolis cottage's great room.
Photograph by Gwin Hunt

FACING PAGE TOP:
Niermann Weeks sconces, mirror and console make an inviting powder room.
Photograph by Gwin Hunt

FACING PAGE BOTTOM:
Soft yellow cabinetry and a chocolate print fabric warm this master bathroom in Great Falls, Virginia.
Photograph by Gwin Hunt

Q&A

More about Leslie ...

WHAT PERSONAL INDULGENCE DO YOU SPEND THE MOST MONEY ON?
eBay; I'm hooked!

WHAT IS THE BEST PART OF BEING AN INTERIOR DESIGNER?
When a sketch becomes a reality.

WHAT IS THE MOST UNIQUE/IMPRESSIVE/BEAUTIFUL HOME YOU'VE BEEN INVOLVED WITH? WHY?
I spent several years working on a very large home in Great Falls. It was a great project because I was able to watch the transition of paper to structure and be a part of each step from the concept to the building and the furnishing of the home.

WHAT IS A SINGLE THING YOU WOULD DO TO BRING A DULL HOUSE TO LIFE?
Start with color and change the elements.

WHAT DO YOU LIKE MOST ABOUT DOING BUSINESS IN YOUR LOCALE?
Annapolis is a fun, casual town with historical elements, beach elements and a much less formal lifestyle than a larger city.

LESLIE HUNT INTERIORS
Leslie Hunt
935 Melvin Road
Annapolis, MD 21403
443.995.3225

Brandel **Johnson**

DESIGNS BY BRANDEL

Brandel Johnson, a Maryland native, began her career in ceramics, receiving her bachelor's degree in art and graduating Magna Cum Laude. This mode of art enabled her to establish a focus on three-dimensional design before turning her attention to interior design. After gaining four years of design experience with a corporation where she received a prestigious award in design, she branched out on her own in 2004 and created Designs by Brandel. In her first year of business, Brandel was invited to participate in the 2005 Baltimore Symphony Orchestra Decorators' Showhouse—a request extended to only the finest and most innovative designers.

Brandel's design philosophy has always been about design tailored to the client. "It's important to get to know your client. Shop with them to see what they gravitate towards, what is meaningful to them and what excites them." Brandel bases her designs on really listening to her clients' needs, even if they can't verbalize them. "If a client says they really like a fabric, I then ask them what they like about it or what they don't like about it. I need to understand what moves them and why," muses the designer. "Before I show them a single thing, we have multiple conversations to see what is really going to make them happy based on

their personality. I am able to listen to their needs and understand what it is they want and provide that for them."

Oftentimes, Brandel feels like a detective with a very specific case to solve; it is her job to figure out the best solutions to the challenges of the design project. For instance, when a client says they would like a romantic bedroom, it is first her job to figure out how they define romantic and translate that into a design tailored to fit their needs.

ABOVE:
The room literally glows with a mix of golden fabrics, exotic woods and metals, such as this 22-karat-gold Venetian Baroque mirror handmade in Italy.
Photograph by Gwin Hunt

FACING PAGE:
Shimmering dupioni silk swags trimmed in delicate knotted ribbon fringe adorn the windows of this graceful dining room, enhancing the lush, romantic feel.
Photograph by Gwin Hunt

She also believes it is her job to keep the client and herself on track with the vision they have arrived at for a room. Her clients may, for example, respond to a formal sofa design that takes them away from the relaxed feeling that the client had expressed they wanted. It is her job to explain why something does or does not work and to let the client know of her concerns. Brandel's greatest concern is maximizing client satisfaction, and she uses optimum communication to achieve this result.

With an emphasis on special touches like custom pieces from local craftsmen and artists, Brandel injects style in the homes she designs, preening every last detail. Brandel once had the pleasure of working on a very memorable project with a couple who had traveled all over the world collecting objects from such diverse places as Africa and Japan. They had a huge collection of coral and lava and wanted a room where they could exhibit objects from all over the world and convey a Hawaiian Asian feel.

Brandel picked up on accessories from their travels to determine elements in the room and united them through a common field of bright color. Using a white leather sectional and covering an antique chair she discovered in their basement with a unique tropical fabric, she created a base for their Hawaiian Asian style.

She then had pillows made in bright tropical colors and blended them with pillows in Indian fabric. She grouped objects by country to give some cohesion to their display. In a boat-shaped basket she found, Brandel placed Japanese fishing balls, lava and shells, creating a Hawaiian beach.

In each project she designs, Brandel's artistic eye doesn't rest until the tiniest details have been placed. It is these final details that she knows will excite her clients and leave them with a personalized, unique feeling in their interiors that they deserve.

ABOVE LEFT:
Bright citrus colors evoke fond memories of this family's former home in Hawaii and provide a backdrop to display collections from around the world.
Photograph by Gwin Hunt

ABOVE RIGHT:
Whimsical touches like a custom portrait of the cherished family cat and a charming mix of patterns keep this formal living room warm and inviting.
Photograph by Gwin Hunt

FACING PAGE TOP:
Dramatic splashes of color and interesting textures play off a base of durable neutral fabrics, making it a stylish yet practical environment for a busy family.
Photograph by Gwin Hunt

FACING PAGE BOTTOM:
The impressive stacked stone fireplace and burnished bronze screen serve as the focal point and were the inspiration for this room's welcoming, elegant style.
Photograph by Gwin Hunt

Q&A

More about Brandel ...

WHAT PERSONAL INDULGENCE DO YOU SPEND THE MOST MONEY ON?
The personal indulgence I spend the most money on is fine dining and wine, although I admittedly spend a ridiculous amount of money on my dogs and cats.

NAME ONE THING MOST PEOPLE DON'T KNOW ABOUT YOU.
Most people don't know that in middle and high school, I was part of a professional magic troupe. In addition to our paid performances, we did free shows at nursing homes.

WHAT IS THE HIGHEST COMPLIMENT YOU'VE RECEIVED PROFESSIONALLY?
The highest compliment I have ever received was during my presentation of a concept for a client's room when she was moved to tears and asked, "How did you read my mind?" Using my intuitive abilities and good listening skills, I am able to glean information from my clients. This information enables me to serve as a translator and ultimately create their ideal environment.

IF YOU COULD ELIMINATE ONE DESIGN TECHNIQUE OR STYLE FROM THE WORLD, WHAT WOULD IT BE?
I would never eliminate any style or technique. I appreciate and respect all styles and find that variety makes the world a much more interesting place. I get excited when I receive the opportunity to work on a project that differs from my personal tastes. It gives me a chance to explore something new.

WHAT COLOR BEST DESCRIBES YOU AND WHY?
Magenta best represents me because it is bold, exciting, surprising and passionate, yet still feminine.

DESIGNS BY BRANDEL
Brandel Johnson
4332 Gilmer Court
Belcamp, MD 21017
410.273.2655
c: 410.459.9354
www.designsbybrandel.com

Soft Touch Photography by Cynthia

135

Sharon **Kleinman**

TRANSITIONS

Sharon Kleinman brings her clients' dreams to fruition in projects ranging from kitchen redesigns to house makeovers to full designs for homes under construction. Sharon brings excitement, passion, expertise and an exacting attention to detail to the design process. Above all, her desire is for her clients to put their personal stamp on their homes. She believes that each interior should reflect the clients' individual taste and personality. To that end, she incorporates sentimental items, hobbies, personal collections and artworks into the overall design scheme because she truly believes that the best interiors evolve over time. "I want my clients to be able to enter any room in their home and feel good about it," Sharon said. "I encourage my clients to think carefully about how they are going to live in each space. Understanding my client's lifestyle is vital to the design process."

Sharon began her design career at the request of friends and neighbors who appreciated her work both in her own home and those close around her. Over a decade later, the business has grown to include new home construction, full-scale renovations and dozens of projects on the board at any given time. Always gaining a great deal of satisfaction from working on a project from the ground

up, Sharon partners with the architect and builder to bring a cohesive design process to the home.

With a design style emphasizing gracious living over ostentation, Sharon's goal is to create rooms that want to be lived in and not merely admired. In her design projects, she strives to create a lifestyle rather than an image. She believes a room should be comfortable while at the same time exuding elegance, style and sophistication. Not only do her design projects maintain a consistent quality, but she preserves a sense of enjoyment for every project. "It's important for the client and me to enjoy not only the end result, but the process as well. By channeling design creativity into a process, the result is a unique interior where the beauty of the room is in the whole and not in a single piece."

ABOVE:
Casual elegance and comfort are achieved with generous yet well-proportioned sofas, a traditional Oushak rug in rich tones and the layering of personal elements of the homeowner.
Photograph by Gwin Hunt

FACING PAGE:
Evocative of a Tuscan villa, a pair of late 18th-century carved Italian chairs, custom sofas and heavy linen draperies create a warm mood. The painting is by the late 19th-century Barbizon school artist Louis Remy Matifas.
Photograph by Gwin Hunt

ABOVE:
Crisp and tailored furniture give intimacy to this large family room. A custom contemporary rug and window treatments balance the room's strong architectural elements. Artwork is by late 19th-century artist Frederick Waugh from the clients' collection.
Photograph by Gwin Hunt

Q&A

More about Sharon ...

WHO HAS HAD THE MOST INFLUENCE ON YOUR CAREER?

My father is a retired architect turned artist whose paintings of landscapes are soothing yet vibrant in their use of color. His exacting attention to detail combined with a passion for his craft has greatly influenced my work.

WHAT ONE ELEMENT OF STYLE OR PHILOSOPHY HAVE YOU STUCK WITH FOR YEARS THAT STILL WORKS FOR YOU TODAY?

Making a room comfortable and enjoyable has as much to do with proportion and scale as it does with pleasing aesthetics achieved through the layering of pattern, texture and color. I infuse my clients' taste with a sense of sophistication, warmth and livability.

WHAT IS THE HIGHEST COMPLIMENT YOU'VE RECEIVED PROFESSIONALLY?

Clients routinely comment that they love spending time in every room of their home. To me that is the ultimate compliment.

WHAT SEPARATES YOU FROM YOUR COMPETITION?

I emphasize client service and attention to detail. In addition, I believe that design should not be a chore; I strive to keep the process enjoyable and fun for all of us. A concerted effort is made to impart my knowledge to my clients, so they are an integral part of the design process.

HAVE YOU BEEN PUBLISHED IN ANY NATIONAL OR REGIONAL PUBLICATIONS? WHICH ONES?

I have been featured in *Washington Home & Design* on numerous occasions. In 2004, I was chosen by the same magazine as one of eight Washington, D.C. area designers to appear in an article focusing on designers' own homes.

TRANSITIONS

Sharon Kleinman
9841 Avenel Farm Drive
Potomac, MD 20854
301.365.5113
www.4transitions.com

ABOVE TOP:
The soft neutral tones of the walls, window treatments and chair fabrics allow the woodwork and carved mantle to take center stage. The painting, by William Mathews, is prized by the owners.
Photograph by Gwin Hunt

ABOVE BOTTOM:
Light-filled and serene, the living room is designed in shades of beiges and creams, punctuated with smoky blue accents. Reflective surfaces of crystal and mirrored glass give sparkle to the space.
Photograph by Gwin Hunt

Victor **Liberatore**

VICTOR LIBERATORE INTERIOR DESIGN

The combined happy accidents of a professor's recognition of innate talent and a subsequent two-dimensional art course led Victor js Liberatore, ASID to make the shift from business administration to interior design. After graduating Magna Cum Laude from the Maryland Institute College of Art and working with firms in Denver and Baltimore, he launched his own design firm in 1981. His fascination with and sensibilities to the potential of forms and their relationship to space have guided his innovative firm and its many creative projects with award-winning results. Victor sees interior design as interior sculpture where a cross-pollenization of ideas creates the essence of each space. His contemporary and transitional environments often include custom cabinetry, stylized furnishings and unique accessories.

A frequent traveler, Victor possesses a particular love of the Caribbean, and its colors and forms find their way into his work. The spatial sense discovered in the horizon line and clouds of Saba east of St. Martin inform, for example, a 970-square-foot condominium where curvilinear lines and stylized abstract clouds created the illusion of expansiveness in a small space.

Each new project and the personalities involved energize this self-described perfectionist and past president of the Maryland Chapter of ASID. With offices in Florida and Baltimore, and projects throughout the northern hemisphere, Victor creates his designs foremost by listening carefully to his clients and making them the essential players on the design team.

ABOVE:
A sunny window-side banquet, with light filtering matchstick blinds affords additional seating for conversation.
Photograph by Alan Gilbert

FACING PAGE:
As a striking graphic, two backlit forms designed as geometric coolie's hats grace the silk matlesse' walls, setting the mood aglow.
Photograph by Alan Gilbert

VICTOR LIBERATORE INTERIOR DESIGN
Victor js Liberatore, ASID
10711 Stevenson Road
Stevenson, MD 21153
410.444.6942
www.victorliberatoreinteriordesign.com

H. Dawn Patrick-Wout

ABOUT INTERIORS

H. Dawn Patrick-Wout, founder and CEO of About Interiors is "changing people's lives one space at a time." As a former therapist, Dawn knows that "people are transformed when their environment mirrors their true inner selves." Her clients, whether residential or commercial, can feel the difference. One homeowner commented, "Dawn seemed to intuitively translate my style and personality into a breathtaking space." Dawn and her team balance timeless beauty, easy elegance and comfort in order to create custom spaces for each client.

In 1994, Dawn set out to establish a design firm that would revolutionize the industry. Today, About Interiors is one of the most widely respected retail stores and design centers in the Mid-Atlantic region, offering a full range of interior design services, workshops, quality furnishings and distinctive accessories.

Dawn's remarkable design acumen is only surpassed by her warm and gregarious spirit, making her one of Washington's favorite design experts. Her designs have already been featured in *Home & Design, The Washington Post, The Baltimore Sun, Northern Virginia Living, Essence Magazine* and HGTV. But even with all this professional success, Dawn's career has only just begun. Driven by a genuine love for people, Dawn continues to beautify spaces as well as lives.

ABOVE:
The focal point of this dining room is the traditional crystal chandelier, which possesses a contemporary flare. The formal dining set includes the square table with glass insert; wenge wood finish and butter-yellow suede chairs. Muted gold walls set a warm and inviting tone for family gatherings.
Photograph by Gwin Hunt

FACING PAGE:
This chocolate brown living room with adjoining dining room features double crown moulding and drapery hardware, both faux painted in antique silver finish. The streamlined sofa and cross-back armchairs, in quilted gold silk, add an air of elegance while the zebra ottoman and shag rug add whimsy. The scroll coffee table is created of hard wood with black enamel finish. Draperies of wide vertical multi-colored stripe silk in chocolate, gold and mustard help to ground and blend each of the interesting facets of the room.
Photograph by Gwin Hunt

ABOVE:
This formal dining room in an old Washington brownstone is warm and inviting with burnt orange walls,
while a contemporary chandelier updates the otherwise traditional space. Soft lines in the oval-backed dining
chairs are the perfect complement to classic mahogany doors and mouldings.
Photograph by Gwin Hunt

Q&A

More about Dawn ...

NAME ONE THING MOST PEOPLE DON'T KNOW ABOUT YOU.
I love cooking almost as much as I love design. I'm never too busy to cook. I could spend all day in the aisles of my local grocery store. I get excited about discovering new and exotic foods, creating new recipes, and yes, of course eating the tasty results.

WHAT BOOK ARE YOU READING RIGHT NOW?
Everything about Papillons ... I adopted Toco (my puppy) last fall, and I'm head over heels in love!

WHAT IS THE HIGHEST COMPLIMENT YOU'VE RECEIVED PROFESSIONALLY?
After a recent workshop, a woman came to me and told me that I had changed her life. She had been battling cancer for four years when a friend invited her to my workshop. She said that it had made her "feel lifted, full of butterflies and warm." She later told her friend that, "Dawn's energy is unbelievable! She makes me want to live!" Even if I never hear another kind word for the rest of my life, those beautiful words are enough to inspire me for a lifetime.

WHAT IS THE SINGLE THING YOU WOULD DO TO BRING A DULL HOUSE TO LIFE?
Add color ... On the walls, in your fabrics and in your accessories! Color is like your personality. It shines through and brings life to your space.

ABOUT INTERIORS
H. Dawn Patrick-Wout
5700-A Sunnyside Avenue
Beltsville, MD 20705
301.220.2811

ABOVE TOP & BOTTOM:
In the adjoining living room, the antique sofa has been restored and reupholstered in a floral Jacobin embroidered silk. Sumptuous shades of gold and burnt orange abound, providing the perfect backdrop for the client's art collection. Tailored balloon valances bathe the bay windows in puddles of striped silk.
Photograph by Gwin Hunt

Kelley **Proxmire**
KELLEY INTERIOR DESIGN SERVICE

With 20 years of experience, Kelley Proxmire has perfected the art of beautiful design, as well as the ability to understand and interpret her clients' vision. The founder of Kelley Interior Design Service, Kelley has become well-known in Washington and across the country for her ability to translate her clients' individual tastes into refined, comfortable and welcoming interiors. She takes great satisfaction in improving her clients' lives by beautifying their surroundings.

Kelley describes her style as Tailored Traditional. She manipulates color, often neutrals and bold primaries, and combines them with her clients' own one-of-a-kind antiques and accessories to create a look unique to each client. "The easiest and best way to bring a dull house to life is with color, still being careful to achieve a flow throughout the house," said the designer.

A testament to her ability to work with color, Kelley recently designed a room in the National Symphony Orchestra Decorators' Showhouse using black, red and white for a bold pop. The room was an awkward space for any designer: a 21-by-9-foot open porch overlooking a parking lot. Kelley upholstered the walls in fresh white indoor/outdoor fabric and swathed the open spaces in dramatic floor-to-ceiling drapes in the same fabric. She grounded the room with a black and white striped carpet, punctuated the airy space with black rattan furniture and black and white pillows in geometric patterns and finished it off in splashes of bright red with pillows and lamp shades. The resulting open-air porch left observers astounded by its fresh, balanced drama.

ABOVE:
Private residence.
Photograph by Angie Seckinger

FACING PAGE:
2003 National Symphony Orchestra Decorators' Showhouse.
Photograph by Ross Chapple

Kelley's paramount attention to detail inspires great trust in her clients and it is this trust that gives full advantage to her creativity. A long-time client of Kelley's began her relationship with the designer with a one-bedroom project. Years later, this relationship has evolved into a friendship and multiple projects including two homes finished down to the smallest accessories.

ABOVE:
Private residence.
Photograph by Angie Seckinger

FACING PAGE:
Private residence.
Photograph by Angie Seckinger

A broad range of clients keep Kelley's work interesting and varied. Working in the Washington, D.C. area, her clients range from professionals, to young couples with children, to adults downsizing after their children have left home. She might be designing a nursery one day and then converting an unused bedroom into an office or living area the next day. The constant variety is a challenge that ensures creative solutions and fresh design.

ABOVE:
Private residence.
Photograph by Angie Seckinger

FACING PAGE TOP:
Private residence.
Photograph by Angie Seckinger

FACING PAGE BOTTOM:
2003 Center for Family Development Showhouse.
Photograph by Ross Chapple

Q & A

More about Kelley ...

YOU WOULDN'T KNOW IT, BUT MY FRIENDS WOULD TELL YOU
I WAS ...
A fan of modern abstract art.

WHAT IS THE BEST PART OF BEING AN INTERIOR DESIGNER?
Having the opportunity to improve your clients' lives by beautifying
their surroundings, updating styles and de-cluttering and providing
practical design solutions for their living needs.

WHO HAS HAD THE BIGGEST INFLUENCE ON YOUR CAREER?
Billy Baldwin, Frances Elkins and Mark Hampton.

WHAT IS A SINGLE THING YOU WOULD DO TO BRING A DULL
HOUSE TO LIFE?
Introduce color while being careful to achieve a flow throughout
the house.

HAVE YOU BEEN PUBLISHED IN ANY NATIONAL OR
REGIONAL PUBLICATIONS?
My work has been published in *Traditional Home, Southern Accents,
Window & Walls, Home & Design* and *Decorator Show Houses* by
Schiffer Books, among others.

KELLEY INTERIOR DESIGN SERVICE
Kelley Proxmire
4519 Wetherill Road
Bethesda, MD 20816
301.320.2109
f: 301.320.2836
www.kelleyinteriordesign.com

Dennese
Guadeloupe Rojas

INTERIORS BY DESIGN

Interior designer Dennese Guadeloupe Rojas took the lemons given to her by a job layoff and didn't just make lemonade; she made her own lemonade stand, Interiors by Design. "I studied interior design in Miami, Florida and did nothing with it. When I was laid off, I was given time to reflect on my life and my passions. It became clear to me that design was my life passion and I could really affect people by manipulating the spaces within their homes," mused the designer. Since 1990, Dennese has been designing medium to large-sized projects. This word-of-mouth operation transitioned into her practice, Interiors by Design, and eventually led to the opening of a retail store, ia, Etc.

Her retail space specializing in accents and accessories enables her to provide clients with just the right rich and unique pieces to complete her exquisite designs. With clients ranging from professional football stars to suburban moms and dads, Dennese, along with her two junior designers and a staff that assists her in putting it all together, enjoys working with a range of styles and budgets, using her ideas and inspirations to make her clients' interior spaces a dream come true.

ABOVE:
A master bathroom complete with all the comforts of a relaxing and invigorating spa. This bathroom was created for the 2005 National Symphony Orchestra Decorators' Showhouse.
Photograph by Gwin Hunt

FACING PAGE:
A space solely dedicated for adults, this room is overwhelmed with the sense of sophistication and elegance for relaxing or for entertaining. This adult space was created for the *Spaces* magazine and Washington Design Center's Spring 2006 Design House.
Photograph by Gwin Hunt

INTERIORS BY DESIGN
Dennese Guadeloupe Rojas
811 Wayne Avenue
Silver Spring, MD 20910
301.495.1030
f: 301.495.6363
www.interiorsbydesignmd.com, www.ia-etc.com

Justine **Sancho**

JUSTINE SANCHO INTERIOR DESIGN, LTD.

J ustine Sancho, founder of Justine Sancho Interior Design, Ltd., dedicates herself and her full-service firm to customer satisfaction. Justine's goal is to develop successful designs that reflect the needs and personality of each client. Communication, patience, attention to detail and quality are the standards of her work which her clients have come to know and expect.

Justine Sancho, who has lived and practiced in the Washington area for over 25 years, is truly leaving her mark on the area. A testament to Justine's contribution to the design community, she was named a Founding Inductee in the Washington Design Center's Hall of Fame of Interior Design. "I love working in this region," said Justine. "This area is convenient to Washington, D.C., New York and Philadelphia. Within a short distance, I can be working on a farmhouse, a townhouse and a city loft, all at the same time. There is also the opportunity to work with a great diversity of clients from all over the world."

Unparalleled customer service is the hallmark for which Justine has become so well-known. Justine works ardently to collect each client's thoughts and tastes and stretch their imaginations in order to create a comfortable, yet timeless interior. Taking advantage of a wide selection of home furnishings including antiques

LEFT:
This gracious living room reflects traditional design that carefully blends antiques with comfortable, transitional furnishings.
Photograph by Lydia Cutter

ABOVE:
This bathed-in-light sophisticated conservatory is an elegant, multi-functional room that reflects the family's lifestyle.
Photograph by Lydia Cutter

ABOVE:
Simple, yet sophisticated and elegant, this transitional-style living room emphasizes bold accent coloring.
Photograph by Lydia Cutter

and custom-designed pieces, she is able to bring uniqueness and variety to each project. Justine communicates closely with clients to clarify objectives and to set priorities. This collaboration ensures that clients avoid costly mistakes and allows both the client and designer to focus effectively on creating exciting interiors that enhance the client's lifestyle.

Justine appreciates the opportunity her profession provides her to help make people's dreams come true. She enjoys utilizing an idea or concept and developing it into a finished product that is both functional and aesthetically pleasing while meeting and oftentimes exceeding her clients' expectations. Even though Justine is an accomplished designer with many accolades to her name, including Washington, D.C.'s highest honor, her greatest joy is still making clients happy.

TOP LEFT:
This living room created for the Washington Design Center's *Rooms of Washington, D.C.*, included oversized art as a unique focal point.
Photograph by Gordon Beall

BOTTOM LEFT:
This master bedroom features a bold, bronze and red color palette and a transitional design.
Photograph by Lydia Cutter

FACING PAGE LEFT:
The dramatic color palette used in this Art Deco-styled ceiling complements an equally bold collection of Clarence Cliff pottery.
Photograph by Gordon Beall

FACING PAGE RIGHT:
Art Deco can be exciting and comfortable.
Photograph by Gordon Beall

Q&A

More about Justine ...

NAME ONE THING MOST PEOPLE DON'T KNOW ABOUT YOU.
I love gardening (often before work, sometimes in my pajamas); from roses to tomatoes, I enjoy watching it all grow—except weeds.

WHAT COLOR BEST DESCRIBES YOU?
Melon; it is a color that can go as deep as terracotta or as soft as pale peach. It is a sophisticated, warm and serene color that leaves an afterglow and displays depth and strength.

YOU WOULDN'T KNOW IT, BUT MY FRIENDS WOULD TELL YOU I AM …
An incurable romantic.

WHO HAS HAD THE BIGGEST INFLUENCE ON YOUR CAREER?
My stepfather's love for beautiful textiles and fashion design were a great influence on me.

WHAT IS THE MOST DIFFICULT TECHNIQUE YOU HAVE USED ON ONE OF YOUR PROJECTS?
We redecorated an existing 1950's half-circle library while saving the exotic wood that encased the walls. Unfortunately, the book cases and part of the wall had extensive water damage. To mask the repairs, we paid tribute to "time." The ceiling was transformed into one half of an enormous, artistically intricate Art Deco clock. The interior view of the clock stretched down the wall to create a canvas illusion, complete with shafts, cogs and gears. This unusual solution reinvigorated an old space and provided a dramatic environment in which the client could enjoy his books and his pottery collection.

JUSTINE SANCHO INTERIOR DESIGN, LTD.
Justine Sancho
10112 Norton Road
Potomac, MD 20854
301.765.6034
f: 301.765.6035
www.justinesancho.com

Skip **Sroka**

SROKA DESIGN INC.

Skip Sroka's first major commission, launched with a recommendation from a tradesman, became a harbinger for his design career. A millwork owner was asked, "Out of all the designers you work with, who really understands what the house is going to look like before it's built?" "Go see Skip Sroka," was his answer, "don't see anyone else."

With a degree from the Cleveland Institute of Art in industrial design, which includes product, car and commercial interior design, Skip enjoys wide regard with tradespeople and clients alike for his understanding of specifications and drawings. His ability to envision and anticipate outcomes with materials and to mold space are what create beautiful backgrounds in his interiors.

Drawn to design for his love of creating environments and seeing results, Skip came to Washington, D.C. in 1984, working first with Victor Shargai before launching Sroka Design in 1987. With 80 percent of the firm's work residential, the practice is unique in that the majority of clients come to him as they are hiring an architect or builder to involve him in work on the plans before ground is ever broken.

At heart practical, Skip plans houses for their maturity so that they continue to function through time for families. He creates carefree environments where clients can come home and relax. His goal with every project is to create a refuge where clients instantly recharge when they enter their space, experiencing the immediate sense of calm, tranquility, and harmony essential to countering today's hectic lifestyles.

ABOVE:
Striking shapes silhouette against the background of this foyer. One can see part of the dining room from the opposite page in the distance. Sroka created the mouldings and floor inlay prior to construction. The large mirror reflects the staircase and the light from the window on the landing above.
Photograph by Timothy Bell

FACING PAGE:
This dining room has many levels of detail that speak eloquently together. The metal studs form a circle in the wool rug. This design is also reflected in the mirror the way the oval sets into the rectangle. The rich brown of the walls creates a background for the crystal and silver chandelier. Silver studs in the aqua blue silk valances lend an unexpected design element. The room is refined and comfortable, an elegant background for the life lived in it.
Photograph by Timothy Bell

This process begins in the planning stages when Skip evaluates client lifestyle, looking at, for example, the intended size of rooms, the number of planned doorways that may interfere with adequate seating in a family room, or a soaring ceiling height that could elicit coldness instead of the desired sense of warmth. Making adjustments to scale, as with the introduction of appropriately sized crown mouldings, can take the cold and big to warm and embracing. Details like the movement of a staircase within a space, the pattern in which tile is laid, the use of wood paneling, draperies and rugs and knowing when to abstain from detail or add it are all key to his process.

Skip is expert at directing the viewer's attention to the strong points of a space, shifting attention away from a room's deficiencies. Working on the renovation of a house which clients built almost 20 years ago and where they were never happy with the functionality of the space, Sroka worked to re-sculpt the interior. He used large cornices to create visual interest and bring down the scale of the high ceilings which made the rooms appear smaller than they actually were. He created a two-

foot band of implied moulding that started at eight feet to counter the verticality and define for the eye the size of the space. Lighting fixtures positioned down into the space create a new sense of intimacy. Leather bound, unusually shaped rugs in geometric designs provided a new vocabulary for the space, adding softness. Creating harmony between all visual elements within a space is key.

ABOVE LEFT:
This renovated kitchen brings the outdoors in. The curved banquette forms an intimate area for dining, a great place to start the day.
Photograph by Timothy Bell

ABOVE RIGHT:
A warm entrance is created with the interplay of art and background color. Sroka did the drawings and overseeing of the mouldings, mantle and lighting. The herringbone floors add a distinctive detail. The curve of the chairs play against the straight lines.
Photograph by Timothy Bell

FACING PAGE:
A standard eight-foot ceiling is given new life by the application of vertical stripes. This provides a visual heightening of the ceiling and a showcasing of the client's art. The fireplace has been fauxed into a metal finish to "kick up" the room.
Photograph by Timothy Bell

With color, for example, which Skip considers the most important decision he makes with each project, he decides which tone will be dominant and will carry the visual weight in a room and which ones will recede to the background. Artwork, fabrics and textiles all factor into building the palette that is unique to each project. "There is a big difference between music and noise," says Sroka, "and it is never more true than in interiors. If a client loves red, for example, you honor that and think of imaginative ways to use the color. Taupey-tan cream upholstery and red walls in living room, for example, with a cream dining room and a red lacquer table are a good solution. A room is like a painting. Some colors must be in the background, others are the features, and they all have to sing in harmony. You can only have one diva singing in a room at a time."

ABOVE:
This room was the 2004 American Society of Interior Designers National Award Winner in conjunction with *Southern Accents* magazine. The oval rug forms a center to the room. The three David Shapiro paintings are hung over the sofa in an unexpected way.
Photograph by Gordon Beall

FACING PAGE LEFT:
Bringing the outdoors into this screened porch while using materials suitable for the outside creates a peaceful and tranquil setting. The rug is made of woven vinyl for carefree living.
Photograph by Gordon Beall

FACING PAGE RIGHT:
A relaxed place near the fireplace composed of stone, bronze, polished steel and leather. Note the custom rug of falling leaves.
Photograph by Gordon Beall

More about Skip ...

WHAT IS ONE THING MOST PEOPLE DON'T KNOW ABOUT YOU?
Reading a book a week is my lifelong habit.

WHAT'S THE HIGHEST COMPLIMENT YOU HAVE RECEIVED PROFESSIONALLY?
When a client says, "Even though you did everything, the house feels like us."

WHAT PERSONAL INDULGENCE DO YOU ENJOY MOST?
Going to a spa, to different masseurs, recharging myself. Pilates classes, and recently, trapeze lessons, are part of that process. I find it exhilarating to think through something new that I've never done before.

WHAT COLOR BEST DESCRIBES YOU?
I love all colors, but see myself as the warm colors aqua, black, cream, and gold.

SROKA DESIGN INC .
Skip Sroka
7307 MacArthur Boulevard, #214
Bethesda, MD 20816
301.263.9100
f: 301.263.9387
www.srokadesign.com

Nadia **Subaran**
Bertin **Radifera**

AIDAN DESIGN

Nadia N. Subaran, a talented and astute native Washingtonian, left D.C. to attend architecture school at The Cooper Union in New York City on a full scholarship. She returned seven years ago, unable to resist the pull of her roots to such a remarkable city. Together, she and her partner and husband, John A. Schmiedigen, created Aidan Design, a full-service design firm devoted to innovative concepts.

Beginning her design journey 12 years ago, Nadia's ever-increasing success with Aidan Design over the last five years is a testament to her exceptional taste and client rapport. Aidan Design is also home to architect Bertin Radifera, whose 20 years of design experience is a great asset to the firm. Collectively as Aidan Design, Nadia and Bertin work with a team of in-house project managers skilled in carpentry, developing projects that result in true customer satisfaction and reflect Aidan's signature styles.

With careful consideration for their clients' needs and desires, Nadia and Bertin work with each client from initial design concept to product selection and procurement, all the way through project completion. The innate ability of both Nadia and Bertin to create balance through simplicity and synergy of geometry, color,

LEFT:
Expansive and strategically designed, this kitchen is infused with natural light, generous countertops and professional appliances. A true cook's kitchen.
Photograph by Fredde Lieberman and Robert Radifera

light and texture place them among the most sought after residential designers in their field. Aidan Design's work has been featured in *Home and Design* magazine, *Washingtonian, Washington Spaces* and *Housetrends*.

Working with clients one-on-one affords Nadia and Bertin the pleasure of undertaking projects with an array of diverse and engaging people and a freedom from convention that few enjoy so thoroughly and thoughtfully.

ABOVE:
This exotic, Asian contemporary kitchen is the showpiece of the home; imaginative and provocative in its use of color and texture.
Photograph by Fredde Lieberman and Robert Radifera

FACING PAGE TOP:
Urban sensibilities lend this kitchen an edgy charm.
Photograph by Fredde Lieberman and Robert Radifera

FACING PAGE BOTTOM:
Dark, rich woods, cool granite countertops, stainless steel appliances and reflective glass tile combine to create this stylish and inviting kitchen.
Photograph by Fredde Lieberman and Robert Radifera

Q&A

More about Nadia ...

DESCRIBE YOUR PERSONAL STYLE.
A mixture of styles leaning towards more minimal detailing and orientation. Less is truly more.

WHAT EXCITES YOU MOST ABOUT BEING A PART OF
SPECTACULAR HOMES?
Being included in a community of great designers!

WHAT IS THE BEST PART OF BEING AN INTERIOR DESIGNER?
Helping clients create and realize great design that reflects their personality and lifestyle.

More about Bertin ...

WHAT ONE PHILOSOPHY HAVE YOU STUCK WITH FOR YEARS THAT STILL WORKS FOR YOU TODAY?
Open up the space and let the house breathe.

WHO HAS HAD THE BIGGEST INFLUENCE ON YOUR CAREER?
Frank Lloyd Wright and Carlo Scarpa.

NAME ONE THING MOST PEOPLE DON'T KNOW ABOUT YOU.
I compose music, but it's for my family's ears only.

AIDAN DESIGN
Nadia Subaran
Bertin Radifera
4701 Sangamore Road, Suite L3
Bethesda, MD 20816
301.320.8735
f: 301.320.8736
www.aidandesign.com

Brad Weesner
BRAD WEESNER DESIGN

Ask Brad Weesner what interior design is all about and he will tell you it is simple; placing beauty in your world makes beauty come to your world—interior design is all about enriching our lives. Brad knows about beauty, as his career has led him from one beautiful place to the next. He began working in private luxury hotels as well as the Ritz Carlton collection of properties, managed luxury corporate real estate and even sold upscale homes in the D.C. area. All of these paths led him to one very defined destination which was the natural culmination of all of his experiences—running his own design firm.

Brad knew from an early age that design was his calling. As a child, his family would enjoy meals at upscale Washington dining rooms and the array of textures and colors always captivated him. Brad now operates one of the most successful design firms in the D.C. area, Brad Weesner Design. Even with his firm's specialty in interior design, many clients come to Brad because of his comprehensive approach. Brad's 24 years in luxury hospitality, real estate management, new home construction and business management provides unparalleled experience in creating customer satisfaction, trust and value. His ability to set high expectations and meet them while also meeting design goals in a sophisticated manner has created long-lasting relationships with many clients. Years of working so intimately with the many facets

of the home building industry have allowed Brad to now provide interior design that is synergistic in its execution.

Embracing the relationships he has built within the design industry, he values the relationships he has built with other designers, superlative tradespeople, supportive representatives from product lines and the people on his team that make his work rewarding and educational on a daily basis.

The evolution of the client relationship and the trust that clients place in him is a great compliment which he cherishes. Brad receives immense satisfaction from working with his clients and believes there are few things more personal than helping someone create beauty within their living environment.

ABOVE:
The detail of this living room shows the soft curve of the sofa's arm repeated throughout the table legs, the cocktail table legs and even the metal floral ornament of the lamp. The backdrop of the large Coromandel screen is supported by concealed boxes. Note the faux finish created to mimic the trim mouldings further minimizing their appearance.
Photograph by Geoffrey Hodgdon

FACING PAGE:
A study in soft repetition, a seafoam and sand scheme conceals a home theater that is hidden behind cornice mouldings and disappears with the touch of a button. The overall lighting scheme produces warm lighting that includes the glow of alabaster and individual lights over the framed prints.
Photograph by Geoffrey Hodgdon

Although at ease working with any design style, Brad's personal style has often been described as a mixture of Transitional, European, Traditional and Eclectic. Brad's rooms are a sophisticated, unique blend of pieces that speak subtly of the mood or place he and the client designate for the space. "Great design is not any one thing that can be put into a category," said the designer, "but the artful combination and placement of colors, style and accessories can take you to a new and beautiful place very quickly."

ABOVE:
This large sun-filled conservatory has commanding views. The goal was to not overdress the windows but let the architecture show through. This mix of pear greens and soft sage greens is accented by soft lilac, truly bringing the outdoors in.
Photograph by Geoffrey Hodgdon

LEFT:
The detail of the conservatory shows the repeated form of the table base and the armchair. The antique lamp is dramatic against the strong architecture and more modern glass table.
Photograph by Geoffrey Hodgdon

FACING PAGE TOP:
This salon is a study in calming colors and classic themes to support the artwork displayed. The upholstered screen is in linen with a two-color toile motif. The scroll arm bench permits views of the water during the day and the fireplace at night.
Photograph by Geoffrey Hodgdon

FACING PAGE BOTTOM:
Note the custom table skirt in silver and the large alabaster lamp intended to carry the weight of the image of the art above. The overall effect is in balance even with a major piece of art.
Photograph by Geoffrey Hodgdon

Q&A

More about Brad ...

WHAT PERSONAL INDULGENCE DO YOU SPEND THE MOST MONEY ON?
I have a passion for beautiful and powerful cars.

NAME ONE THING MOST PEOPLE DON'T KNOW ABOUT YOU.
I love to tell jokes and recant wonderfully humorous stories. The art of conversation and engaging another's visualization is something I love to do.

WHAT COLOR BEST DESCRIBES YOU AND WHY?
Pale mineral blues because they are so calming and peaceful and fresh cucumber greens because they stir my imagination.

YOU WOULDN'T KNOW IT, BUT MY FRIENDS WOULD TELL YOU I WAS...
Crazy in love with my dog Schofield. My partner, Mike, and I spent a lot of time researching the breed and looking for the very best breeders of Soft Coated Wheaten Terriers. From his birth we took a lot of care to do all the right things, including puppy kindergarten and training. He is such a gentleman and he is truly one of the best examples of his breed. We keep him in a full show coat with weekly grooming, which he just sees as play time. He even likes to have his face washed after dinner.

WHAT IS A SINGLE THING YOU WOULD DO TO BRING A DULL HOUSE TO LIFE?
Lighting, lighting, lighting (after color, of course).

WHO HAS HAD THE BIGGEST INFLUENCE ON YOUR CAREER?
Justine Sancho, one of Washington D.C.'s most venerable and respected interior designers. I will never forget the first time I saw one of her rooms and immediately had to research the person who had designed that beautiful space. Her ability to quickly convey a point while still being warm and likeable speaks to her many years of working with Washington's elite. She gives back to the design community in many ways by doing charitable work and mentoring designers new to the field.

BRAD WEESNER DESIGN
Brad Weesner
Everedy Square, 6 North East Street
Frederick, MD 21701
301.631.0990
f: 301.631.0018
www.bradweesnerdesign.com

DESIGNER: Marlies Venute, Marlies Venute Interiors, Inc., *Page 231*

DESIGNER: Victoria Sanchez, Interiors by Victoria Sanchez, *Page 209*

DESIGNER: Michael Roberson, Michael Roberson Interior Design, *Page 203*

Northern Virginia

Jeff **Akseizer**

AKSEIZER DESIGN GROUP

Imagine the elegance of a Park Avenue pied-à-terre, a breezy beach cottage on Nantucket's coast and the 1940's set of "The Great Gatsby" film; this best describes the work of Akseizer Design Group. The firm's principal, Jeff Akseizer, is an effervescent blend of talent and Washington, D.C.'s rising star. He founded his firm in 2001 as a residential interior designer, putting his true gift for visualizing and creating great interior spaces to work.

Jeff was born to be an interior designer with his photographic memory and love of architecture. As a boy he absorbed the culturally-rich experiences of growing up on the outskirts of New York City, but his parents were his greatest influence giving him the philosophy to believe in "possibilities" and do everything with good humor. Today, it is this success secret that allows Jeff to accomplish what some designers would deem impossible.

Jeff works with each client to grasp their vision and discuss ideas, desires and needs. He underscores listening as the most important aspect of the designer-client relationship. His uncanny ability to know a homeowner inside and out during the design process makes working with Jeff a delight for both parties and ensures an enriching experience. He often gives "homework," sending his clients

on field trips to find art and accessories with meaning to bring a very personal feel to the space they call home. His passion then becomes one with the client and the work begins.

Most often at his side is his associate, Maria Abapolnikova, who shares his love for classic, sophisticated design serving some of Washington's most high-profile people. Looking at a space as if it were a Hollywood set is the primary way that his studio approaches interior design work, whether a luxury condo, entire home, room or basement space. You may see four walls, a corner and a door, but Jeff sees no obstruction to envisioning the final design and always focuses on the possibilities.

ABOVE:
Antique Indonesian fishing baskets hang as pendant lights above a solid cherry bar, adding a Costa Rican influence to the lower level recreation room, media room and library in Mclean, Virginia.
Photograph by Abby Greenawalt

FACING PAGE:
The Darrel Chair designed by Deborah Gore Dean complements this intimate dining room table. Stucco textured walls and terracotta floors with tangerine trees in 19th-century Italian urns create a warm, rustic ambiance.
Photograph by Abby Greenawalt

Traveling the world in his mind, he brings fresh ideas to create a customized interior based on client direction. He visualizes the final outcome and proceeds confidently to communicate the interior concept, first determining budgetary parameters and promising to exceed expectations.

Jeff has an affinity for organic materials and weaves them into many interior projects. It is this trademark element of style which gives a subtle, natural impression to anyone who enters a space finished by his team of talent. His interiors evoke a true organic feeling through the use of rare species of woods, exceptional millwork and cabinetry, pure linen and bamboo elements.

Jeff also believes that effective lighting is the key to every room, and his designs reflect strategic use of light to create an ambiance. He also mixes old and ultra new,

integrating antiques and unusual pieces of custom furniture into a space. Borrowing from the past and adapting to today's living is a design challenge that Jeff thrives on. Always referring back to basic design principles and a "less is more" design attitude, sprinkled with the magic of Hollywood imagination, Akseizer Design Group is a rare find.

ABOVE:
Modern glamour turns a traditional living room into a naturally sophisticated style using velvet and linens, an antique zebra hide,18th-century urns atop the mantle and a drizzle of crystals just above the fireplace.
Photograph by Abby Greenawalt

FACING PAGE:
Guests are welcomed through traditional French doors into the gallery area where an antique bench and colorful fabrics create a dreamy resting spot.
Photograph by Abby Greenawalt

More about Jeff ...

NAME ONE THING MOST PEOPLE DON'T KNOW ABOUT YOU.
I love Broadway show tunes because I'm originally a New Yorker.

WHAT IS THE BEST PART OF BEING A DESIGNER?
Being asked to enter into someone's most personal and precious space, assisting them with enhancing the way they live and getting a glimpse into their dreams.

WHAT PERSONAL INDULGENCE DO YOU SPEND THE MOST MONEY ON?
Accessories and antiques, as they create the personality of a space. Beyond giving form and function, they can transport you to great places with their story.

WHAT COLOR BEST DESCRIBES YOU AND WHY?
Orange and fuschia are two of my favorites because they always make you smile. I'm known to inspire a few laughs and make the design process fun.

AKSEIZER DESIGN GROUP
Jeff Akseizer
1401 Chain Bridge Road
McLean, VA 22101
703.288.9488
f: 202.315.3014
www.akseizerdesign.com

Robin Bergeson

BERGESON DESIGN STUDIO

Robin Bergeson, ASID acquired her design and arts sensibility by environmental osmosis. Raised by an artist, Robin absorbed from her talented mother, who was proficient in many media, an appreciation and understanding for beauty that flows through the interiors she creates and art collections she helps clients build.

Born in Missouri, raised on the East Coast, Robin was living in Monterey, California pursuing a career in social work with a focus in women's issues, when an observant friend suggested Robin turn the talents she had used to create her own unique living environment to the field of interior design.

Extensive residence abroad in Japan and Spain followed her studies at Monterey Peninsula College. Her warm style combines elements of the simple clean aesthetic discovered in Asia with the layered character and comfortable sense of history experienced in continental Europe. Robin's passion for melding these diverse influences gives her a design agility that allows her to create environments that uniquely reflect the clients and their lifestyles and experiences.

"Warm" is the adjective most consistently used to describe Robin's projects. A passion for deep color and an interest in texture discovered through rich fabrics

find expression in her work. For Robin the experience of designing an environment is all about working with a client and getting them where they want to be. She finds that fabric can provide a way into the project for her and the client. She takes a hands-on approach, arriving at the first appointment with a plethora of fabric samples to experience and spark responses. Through conversation she discovers more—is this a person who leads a simple life, a hectic life with no time of their own to focus on the home, or one who owns a collection they are proud of? Are they family centered, do they entertain? Potential palette cues are discovered by observing the colors clients surround themselves with, the colors they wear. Together they go through magazines to respond to colors and environments. With

ABOVE:
An artist's home blends her love of color with her Oriental collection and inherited antique chairs. The interior is updated with contemporary fabric, a glass table and a Murano glass light fixture.
Photograph by Gwin Hunt

FACING PAGE:
The artist's art collection provided inspiration for her Georgetown condo.
Photograph by Gwin Hunt

the client, Robin begins to develop a look that cues from the conversation, leading her to design solutions that reflect their unique situation.

As residents of a city at the forefront of trends, Robin finds Washington clients are willing to experiment and take the risks that lead to incredible rooms. Recent projects include a family room for a native Portuguese client who wanted an Old World look that would work with today's technology. Robin used a lush hand, creating a color palette that conveys the patina and warmth of age, supported by the warmth of texture provided by velvets and leather. 17th and 18th-century reproduction furnishings support the desired look but provide durability and the spaciousness to accommodate a 21st-century entertainment center. For the dining room of another home, faux finishers experimented with a recently-learned technique to create copper metallic walls, combined with a ceiling painted in layered tones of copper, brown and blue.

Robin's frequent travels—just back from London, a trip is planned for the Caribbean in the spring and for Italy next year—find their way into her work, both as inspiration and as finds for current projects. She loves melding the old and new, and possesses the eye for artfully blending it all.

TOP RIGHT:
Atmosphere and a touch of whimsy were created by the choice of lighting for an Old World dining experience.
Photograph by Gwin Hunt

BOTTOM RIGHT:
Warmth and livability are created for this family room through a melding of Old World charm and today's comfort.
Photograph by Gwin Hunt

FACING PAGE LEFT:
The seashore was the influence for this elegant, romantic and welcoming dining room.
Photograph by Gwin Hunt

FACING PAGE RIGHT:
The tone was set for the rest of the house through the rich character here in the foyer.
Photograph by Gwin Hunt

ABOVE:
A pillow-filled window seat, soft wall treatments, hand-painted and applied medallions, hand-painted coffered
ceiling and chandelier combine to make a most romantic library.
Photograph by Gwin Hunt

FACING PAGE LEFT:
Quiet corner.
Photograph by Gwin Hunt

FACING PAGE RIGHT:
A touch of drama.
Photograph by Gwin Hunt

More about Robin ...

WHAT WORD BEST DESCRIBES YOUR PERSONAL DESIGN VISION?
Eclectic. I love blending the old and the new, contemporary and older pieces.

WHAT PERSONAL INDULGENCE DO YOU ENJOY?
Frequent travel. It provides the inspiration and new discoveries that influence my work.

WHAT IS ONE THING THAT PEOPLE DON'T KNOW ABOUT YOU?
I'm a skilled flamenco dancer, a talent developed in Spain.

WHAT IS THE ONE THING YOU WOULD DO TO BRING A DULL HOUSE TO LIFE?
Paint! New color adds incredible life to an environment for very little cost.

WHAT IS THE HIGHEST COMPLIMENT YOU HAVE RECEIVED PROFESSIONALLY?
When a new client observed in my work the many layers and true understanding seen in each of my projects.

BERGESON DESIGN STUDIO
Robin Bergeson, ASID
20818 Confidence Court
Ashburn, VA 20147
703.723.7557

Barry Dixon
BARRY DIXON, INC.

Known throughout the country, Barry Dixon is a designer whose philosophy is based upon the integrity of good design. Widely appreciated, he has been named to *House Beautiful's* List of Top Designers in America for five consecutive years. With degrees including art history and design and a childhood filled with international travel, Barry's worldly, sophisticated aesthetic sense is the hallmark for which he has become so acclaimed.

Bitten by the design bug at an early age, he vividly recalls minute aspects of his parent's restoration of a historic home with a Memphis decorator when he was six or seven years old. Barry had ample opportunity to see the process repeated as his father's position with a foreign corporation took the family to ever more exotic locales.

Setting up house in South Africa or the South Pacific, dragging things home from Korea and India, Barry unwittingly absorbed a "global aesthetic sensibility" that celebrates not only cultural differences but similarities. He believes that wherever they come from, fabrics, patterns, furnishings and art are merely man's interpretations of the glorious natural world around him. It is this common organic

inspiration that allows their happy coexistence in the modern interior. Furthermore, since nature has "always been" creative mankind's inspiration, then this organic thread becomes the means to pull all the "beautiful bits" of aesthetic history, the styles and periods, into one coherent whole. By divine default, this process distills the most blessed result—timelessness, that when layered with other paramount necessities such as comfort and practicality, form and proportion, and seasoned with others like personality, nuance, wit and whimsy, approaches an infallible formula for "avoiding the formulaic."

Observing that there are three voices within each design project, Barry lends credence to each one. First the homeowners—who are they? How do they live? What makes them happy? Then, there is the voice of the house itself. What period

ABOVE:
A simple hall becomes a study of opposites: hard/soft, convex/concave, clean/ornate, neutral/colored.
Photograph by Gordon Beall

FACING PAGE:
A harmonized blend of old and new effect a timelessness in this corner near the sea.
Photograph by Gordon Beall

is it? Where is it located? Is it new? What is its history? What will it be comfortable with? And finally the voice of the designer, which has led the client here in the first place. Only by listening carefully to the home and homeowner and by being true to his inner voice does Barry feel he can "put the puzzle together" for his clients and achieve the premium end result—a bespoke interior that reflects the people who live there.

ABOVE:
Romantic woodland elements set a dramatic stage in this Virginia dining room.
Photograph by Tria Giovan

FACING PAGE:
Organic elements, blended stones and woods, lend a rustic formality to this Montecito living room.
Photograph by Gordon Beall

ABOVE:
A reception area in a Virginia country house feels vital and fresh with traditional overtures.
Photograph by Tria Giovan

FACING PAGE TOP:
A woodsy foyer bears testament to the myriad influences of Craftsman style.
Photograph by Tria Giovan

FACING PAGE BOTTOM:
Mixing tribal and traditional styles with an earthy "Arts & Craftsiness" yields this cozy realm.
Photograph by Gordon Beall

Q&A

More about Barry ...

WHAT PERSONAL INDULGENCE DO YOU SPEND THE MOST MONEY ON?
Right now we spend a lot of time working on our farm. The restoration of the barn, a new tractor, exotic laying hens, a new hen house, livestock, feed and all the other things that come along with life in the country seem to add up fiscally.

NAME ONE THING MOST PEOPLE DON'T KNOW ABOUT YOU.
Though my Southern roots run deep, I've lived all over the world.

WHAT COLOR BEST DESCRIBES YOU AND WHY?
Dark brown comes to mind; basic, earthy, malleable and I like to think, easy to work with.

WHAT IS THE HIGHEST COMPLIMENT YOU'VE RECEIVED PROFESSIONALLY?
That our work is elegant yet approachable, livable and, of course, we're always flattered when editors publish our designs.

WHAT ONE ELEMENT OF STYLE HAVE YOU STUCK WITH FOR YEARS THAT STILL WORKS FOR YOU TODAY?
Mix it up!

WHAT IS THE MOST BEAUTIFUL HOME YOU'VE BEEN INVOLVED WITH AND WHY?
Maybe my own home is the most beautiful because it's so personal and familiar.

BARRY DIXON, INC
Barry Dixon
Elway Hall
8394 Elway Lane
Warrenton, VA 20186
540.341.8501
f: 540.341.8502
www.barrydixon.com

Susan Gulick

SUSAN GULICK INTERIORS

Susan Gulick discovered her creative expression in interior design through the fine arts. With a degree in painting and credentials to teach from the University of Michigan, she returned to school in her mid-30s to complete a degree in design. The burgeoning field presented a perfect fit for her strengths of creativity, problem solving and technical skills.

In business since 1987, Susan builds livable interiors in layers just as an artist builds a painting on a canvas. Her full-service practice, based in Northern Virginia, works with new and renovated homes. Homeowners find that Susan's designs connect at every stage of a project; from early selections of lighting and plumbing fixtures, to the paint on the walls; from customized window treatments and millwork, to the thoughtfully selected and placed furnishings, accessories and artwork.

Color is this designer's love and strength. Her innate sense for the medium, honed by her education in the fine arts, creates a harmonious flow that modulates from room to room. She begins with a dominant tone and layers related shades throughout the house to create a connected feeling. Clients discover her carefully constructed colorways give them great flexibility and contribute to the functionality

and comfortable feel of their homes. Furnishings can be rearranged, even moved from room to room, and still the pieces come together with ease.

The idea for a color palette can be inspired by many different things such as current design trends, a favorite work of art, or even through observing a client's choice in personal dress. The palette is often then refined to fit the client's desired environment.

Susan feels the selection of art at the end of a project is the element that can bring the whole together. At home and in her travels she constantly looks at art and visits galleries, noting artists whose vision inspire her and may be appropriate for future projects.

ABOVE:
Beginning with the clients' antique sideboards, Susan designed this elegant dining room by layering a mix of traditional and contemporary elements.
Photograph by Judy Davis, HDPhoto

FACING PAGE:
Stunning yet inviting describes this renovated family room. Full-height draperies accentuate the palladian windows and the height of the space. The warm color palette and comfortable furnishings keep it intimate.
Photograph by Judy Davis, HDPhoto

But for Susan design is not only about aesthetics. The designer's principal challenge is to create aesthetically pleasing solutions that still work functionally, so you can go about living—with the kids, the cats, the dogs—and still have an environment that contributes to the reduction of the stress of daily life. Susan rises to this challenge, in every job, to arrive at the perfect answer that works for each client.

ABOVE:
An unusual color combination of apricot and blue topaz with neutrals unifies separate but complementary living spaces.
Photograph by Judy Davis, HDPhoto

FACING PAGE TOP:
A mixture of textures and rich colors were selected to create a soothing master retreat.
Photograph by Judy Davis, HDPhoto

FACING PAGE BOTTOM:
Challenged with a face lift to this living space, Susan incorporated the clients' favorite dining room table with contemporary furnishings. Bold colors were drawn from the artwork adding a playful element to a sophisticated redo.
Photograph by Judy Davis, HDPhoto

Q&A

More about Susan ...

WHAT IS THE SINGLE THING YOU WOULD DO TO BRING A DULL HOUSE TO LIFE?
Add artwork to the walls.

WHAT COLOR BEST DESCRIBES YOU?
Blue: Calm, cool and self-assured.

WHAT SEPARATES YOU FROM YOUR COMPETITORS?
Sophisticated livable interiors. People say that my houses are so inviting and comfortable they could just pack their bags and move in.

WHAT ONE ELEMENT IN YOUR DESIGN PHILOSOPHY HAVE YOU USED CONSISTENTLY THROUGHOUT YOUR CAREER?
Simplicity of detail. I believe that less is more, which is reflected in my consistent, clean-lined approach.

SUSAN GULICK INTERIORS
Susan Gulick
12021 Sunset Hills Road Suite 200
Reston, VA 20190
703.674.0332

Vivianna **Irizarri**

IK&F, INC.

Vivianna Irizarri, managing partner of the IK&F Design Disciplines, is not your typical designer. Offering design services with her own retail store and custom millwork facility, Vivianna offers her clients total design services. Clients are able to visit her store and facility and experience firsthand the goods and services she so uniquely offers. Managing the retail division of IK&F called Cache Furnishings, she carries over 1,000 binders with offerings in furniture, lighting, art and accessories, offering her clients "T.I.E."—Total Identity Enhancement.

Vivianna began her career as a business person working for advertising agencies in New York after attending Parsons School of Design. She found graphic design and art direction too limiting so she followed her strong desire to move to the three-dimensional realm. Vivianna's mother, a couturier, had always inspired Vivianna creatively, so she decided it was time to put this creativity into action.

Her introduction to the design business began in 1997 with her purchase of a sign company with millwork capability where she began to design furniture and custom home built-ins. She began to design many interior projects for her friends and discovered she could express herself creatively while satisfying her clients. She

brought a managing partner into the business who was trained in Florence, Italy, to assure the highest quality woodworking and architectural design.

Now, IK&F is flourishing—with 21 full-time and three part-time employees, Vivianna has built a culture based on the foundation of how she does business. Vivianna always stresses that the business isn't about her; it's about what she believes in and what she's passionate about.

ABOVE:
This enclosed dining room measures 11' x 14' and is designed with a faux-glazed bronze finish wall with an amber Art Deco chandelier and modern wrought iron floor lights.
Photograph by Bob Narod

FACING PAGE:
Classical architecture is celebrated with these formal mouldings and arched windows and is complemented by a warm butter-colored wall paint. Extraordinary opulence abounds with this "in-style and timeless classic look." Sumptuous sofas, lush window treatments and ambient lighting combined with the urns reflect the client's personal taste.
Photograph by Bob Narod

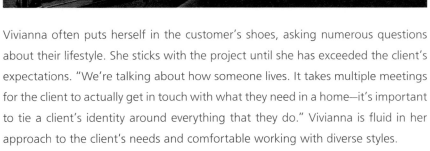

Vivianna often puts herself in the customer's shoes, asking numerous questions about their lifestyle. She sticks with the project until she has exceeded the client's expectations. "We're talking about how someone lives. It takes multiple meetings for the client to actually get in touch with what they need in a home—it's important to tie a client's identity around everything that they do." Vivianna is fluid in her approach to the client's needs and comfortable working with diverse styles.

A unique offering of the business is Cache-on-Wheels, where table-top home accessories, accent furniture, wall décor and art and window treatments are brought directly to the client's home so they can be experienced before a commitment is made. Vivianna is adept at working with the materials her clients already own and advising them on supplementing their environment to achieve the desired look and to make the room complete. Working with products in her store, she uses her fresh perspective to advise clients how to pull the room together, adjust the color palette, rearrange the room and pull everything together to make a room complete.

Vivianna travels extensively, collecting furnishings, art and accessories for her inventory that she discovers amongst the streets of the cities she visits. She seeks out artisans, exploring their back rooms for overlooked treasures; these items often speak to current and potential projects. Most recently, she discovered a number of gold-leafed trays and paintings and purchased a number of reproductions from

ABOVE LEFT:
Selected use of mirrored furnishings makes this living room light and airy. The gold mirror screen, cocktail table and end table lamp are accompanied by a whimsical driftwood finished mahogany chair and table-top water-illusion flower arrangement.
Photograph by Bob Narod

ABOVE RIGHT:
Vivianna suggested that the client install the large Oriental screen on the wall to bring out the multi-layered materials within it.
Photograph by Bob Narod

ABOVE:
Vivianna designed this bedroom for Isabella, the youngest member of the family. The silk bed canopy embraces
this hand-painted Amy Howard queen-size bed and patina nightstand. The small but dramatic room is completed
with the final touches of eggshell blue walls and a suede crimson duvet with accent throw pillows.
Photograph by Bob Narod

an engraving workshop while in Florence, Italy. She finds these treasure hunts invigorating; she has avidly studied periods in art history and furniture, enabling her to work comfortably by combining different periods.

Designing for the genre of our times, Vivianna looks to create designs that possess longevity and avoid looking outdated. She is currently inspired by bringing an individualized artistic touch to furniture with wall frescoes and engravings. Her approach is forward-looking; she is progressive in her vision and often anticipates trends that have not yet penetrated the general market.

ABOVE:
The Venetian wall is complemented by a side console and clock manufactured by Artifacts and an old Framboisette poster purchased in France. The built-in contrasts the owners' books and accessories purchased on trips to New York and Europe.
Photograph by Bob Narod

LEFT:
This queen-size bed with leather headboard inserts by J.D. Chamberlain along with chair and nightstands made by Environment are perfectly scaled furnishings for this small master bedroom.
Photograph by Bob Narod

FACING PAGE:
Soaring ceilings and a dramatic cedar balcony adorn this beautiful family room, reflecting the homeowner's style and taste. Checkered pillows by The John Rogers Collection, hand-embroidered small pillows by English Garden, cocktail table by Swaim and upholstering by Robert Allen complete the design.
Photograph by Bob Narod

Q&A

More about Vivianna ...

WHAT IS THE BEST PART OF BEING AN INTERIOR DESIGNER?
I am never limited by the interior design spaces of a home. My best home projects have been ones that have challenged me with unusual architectural elements and odd room shapes.

WHAT IS THE HIGHEST COMPLIMENT YOU'VE RECEIVED PROFESSIONALLY?
I've been honored with many awards in my career, but the highest compliment I've ever received professionally was from friends who were speaking about me at a party and I happened to hear what they were saying. It is humbling to think that they see me as a person who is "down to earth and unpretentious."

WHO HAS HAD THE BIGGEST INFLUENCE ON YOUR CAREER?
I have to say it was my mother. She pushed me to challenge my talents and worked hard to get me through the School of Art and Design High School and Parsons School of Design. She always said that "you can be the most creative person on this earth, but if you have no business sense of how to manage your talents, you won't go very far in your career."

YOU CAN TELL I LIVE IN THIS LOCALE BECAUSE...
I have the freedom and financial independence to express my creativity and business skills, unlike any other city such as New York, where I am originally from. It is rare to have the ability to be creative and successful in business at the same time.

IK&F, INC.
Vivianna Irizarri
14100 Parke Long Court, Suite C
Chantilly, VA 20151-1644
703.378.9100
f: 703.378.9400
www.ik-f.com

Michael **Roberson**

MICHAEL ROBERSON INTERIOR DESIGN

Recognized as one of Washington's most influential designers, Michael Roberson is best known for her innovative approach to layering and blending contemporary furnishings with unique objects and antiques. With an emphasis on openness and light, her work captures an unusual sense of calm and harmony.

Michael's lifelong immersion in art and design began when, as a young child, she was the winner of a Scholastic Art Competition scholarship to the museum school at the Museum of Fine Arts, Houston. After extensive study in fine arts, she was drawn to the field of interior design as her focus.

Michael's training in art informs her work, bringing an understanding of scale, proportion, volume and space to designing interiors. "Developing a well-balanced room is like creating a painting," says Michael. "I visualize the whole space as a composition rather than as a collection of separate items."

For Michael the design process starts with identifying an environment that will fulfill her clients' needs. This motivation becomes the impulse on which she builds livable, beautiful interiors. Combining a dynamic aesthetic with the comforts of home is her ultimate goal. Whether Michael is designing interiors for a new contemporary home overlooking Rock Creek Park or a 1920's Colonial on Kalorama Road, she is drawn to good architecture and the opportunity to create spaces for living. Michael's designs convey timeless style in clean, harmonious, light-filled spaces that also serve as functional areas for living and working.

ABOVE:
Antique black Chinese chest, African carving and Sylvia Bower porcelain.
Photograph by Gordon Beall

FACING PAGE:
Custom sectional designed by Michael Roberson. Donghia Eaton chair, Cassina coffee tables, and Willem de Looper painting complete the room.
Photograph by Gordon Beall

She continues to be intrigued by the challenge of a project's limitations and the opportunity to create spaces that positively influence those who experience them. With an extraordinary ability to transform difficult and limiting floor plans into interesting areas that are surprising and unexpected, Michael is known to be one of the most creative and resourceful designers in the Washington metro area.

For over 20 years, Michael has built upon her reputation and expanded her firm, Michael Roberson Interior Design, receiving recognition from numerous design institutions and publications. Awarded the 1999 Designer of Distinction Award by the ASID, Metro Washington Chapter, and an inaugural member of the Washington Design Hall of Fame, her work has appeared in the pages of *House Beautiful, Traditional Home, Southern Accents* and *The Washington Post*, among others. Her participation in 12 area designer showhouses was recognized in 1994 and in 1998 by *House Beautiful* as one of the "10 Best Showhouse Rooms in America."

ABOVE:
A Niermann Weeks console, a Chinese bowl and beveled mirrors create a serene composition.
Photograph by Gordon Beall

FACING PAGE:
Loveseat and steel game table designed by Michael Roberson. Noguchi lamps, Hans Wegner chairs and custom, woven straw folding screen.
Photograph by Gordon Beall

ABOVE:
Rodgers and Goffigan linen velvet on chairs, Wade Hoefer painting, linen lamp shades and "Michael" table from David Iatesta.
Photograph by Gordon Beall

FACING PAGE TOP:
Post and Beam architecture. Pair of antique Japanese chests, shoji screen on window and pair of Holtkotter bedside lamps complement this space.
Photograph by Gwin Hunt

FACING PAGE BOTTOM:
A Fritz Scholder etching anchors a tabletop arrangement.
Photograph by Floyd Roberson

Q&A

More about Michael ...

YOU CAN TELL THAT I LIVE IN WASHINGTON D.C. BECAUSE ...
We discuss politics at dinner parties!

WHAT IS THE HIGHEST COMPLIMENT YOU HAVE
RECEIVED PROFESSIONALLY?
Praise from my clients.

WHAT PERSONAL INDULGENCES DO YOU ENJOY?
Books, wine and the garden.

WHAT IS THE MOST UNIQUE/IMPRESSIVE/BEAUTIFUL HOME YOU
HAVE BEEN INVOLVED WITH?
It always seems to be the one we are working on at the time. I'm
fortunate enough to have worked in many unique and
beautiful homes.

THE BOOK MICHAEL IS READING NOW ...
Eric Larson's *The Devil in the White City* and, because it is winter
now, a pile of gardening catalogues.

WHAT IS ONE THING MOST PEOPLE DON'T KNOW ABOUT YOU?
My granddaughter, who thinks it is very funny, will tell you that I
almost always cry when I see children perform.

WHAT ONE ELEMENT OF STYLE OR PHILOSOPHY HAVE YOU STUCK
WITH FOR YEARS THAT STILL WORKS?
To make sure that each room has "generations," furnishings from
different eras.

MICHAEL ROBERSON INTERIOR DESIGN
Michael Roberson, ASID
4320 Lorcom Lane
Arlington, VA 22207
703.527.9010
f: 703.276.0091
www.michaelroberson.com

Victoria **Sanchez**

INTERIORS BY VICTORIA SANCHEZ

Victoria Sanchez, founder and owner of Victoria Sanchez Interiors, is a believer in design for the masses. She wants people to know that good design does not require a million-dollar budget; good design can be found in hand-me-down furniture if that is all there is to work with. It is easy to see in her work that Victoria's basic design principles are timeless and sensible. No matter what she is given to work with, Victoria is the type of designer who can make a house into a comfortable, livable home.

For many years, Victoria has based her practice on being sensible about design. "Whether you are a multimillionaire with an unlimited budget or a single mother just starting out, you still need sensible design work. Balance, scale and proportion are three elements that are critical to each design, no matter the environment or design scheme," said Victoria. This notion first became obvious to her at the age of 23 when she purchased her first home. Despite the fact that her home was decorated using furniture and accessories from second-hand stores, everyone she invited into her home would comment on its excellent design. Victoria knew from that point on that sensibility and comfort are the keystones of design.

As a child, Victoria would visit her grandmother's home in the country and witness the constant changes she made to her interior space which, even at a young age, Victoria felt were the apotheosis of good design. Victoria first became educated in design from the trips she and her grandmother would take to antique stores where her grandmother would teach her the finest details of design: how to read the backs of china, choose the right upholstery or follow the grain of a fabric. The business side of Victoria's designer/entrepreneur persona was inspired by her father, an astute businessman who instilled his business savvies in his children.

ABOVE:
A family antique table anchors a large-scaled oil painting and displays family photos, which Victoria insists should be displayed throughout a home.
Photograph by Ross Chapple

FACING PAGE:
The dark brown walls give this living room the sophistication it deserves, while the accents of citrus green found in the fabrics and accessories keep the design fresh.
Photograph by Ross Chapple

Q&A
More about Victoria ...

WHAT PERSONAL INDULGENCE DO YOU SPEND THE MOST MONEY ON?
Shoes; they are such an easy addiction.

NAME ONE THING MOST PEOPLE DON'T KNOW ABOUT YOU.
I am very much a homebody. I am very domestic and I love to cook, garden and entertain.

WHAT COLOR BEST DESCRIBES YOU AND WHY?
Pinks and purples because they are a little showy, a little fun and they are fiesta colors. I am Latina, so I have a party streak in me that these colors reflect.

WHAT IS THE HIGHEST COMPLIMENT YOU'VE RECEIVED PROFESSIONALLY?
The best compliment is being told that I know what a client wants before they know themselves. When I meet someone, I try to interpret what they want, even if they don't know what they want yet. It is such a joy to be able to hit something for them before they can even put it into words. I am immensely gratified when I hear, "That's it. That's what I want."

HAVE YOU BEEN PUBLISHED IN ANY NATIONAL OR REGIONAL PUBLICATIONS? WHICH ONES?
I am currently finishing a chapter in the book *Casa y Comunidad* about adding Latino flavor to interiors. This book about the Latino home industry is being put together in partnership with the National Homebuilders Association and is geared towards builders, architects and the design community to demonstrate how Latinos have an enormous influence on the home-buying community.

WHAT SEPARATES YOU FROM YOUR COMPETITION?
My work is unique and sought after because I am skilled at layering many colors, textures and fabrics in one room without it appearing confusing. I like to layer interesting combinations of color and pattern to make a unique room. I'm not afraid of pushing color and texture ... sometimes it just works.

INTERIORS BY VICTORIA SANCHEZ
Victoria Sanchez
2611 Childs Lane
Alexandria, VA 22308
703.966.2181
f: 703.360.0434

Victoria has an appreciation for several styles including Sante Fe, French Country and Shabby Chic, to name a few. As an interior designer, she is able to work with all of these different styles of décor. "Often I will fall in love with a new fabric and I will think, 'It may not be perfect for my home, but it will be perfect for someone's home.'" Victoria finds immense excitement in trying different things and experimenting with new techniques. That is why she loves interior design; the new challenges she faces with each project make the business exciting and exhilarating.

ABOVE:
Victoria's touch is evident in this lady's shoe closet from the pretty pink fabrics to the beautiful hand-painted englomeise-style floor mirror.
Photograph by Gordon Beall

FACING PAGE:
The epitome of elegance: metallic-glazed walls reflecting the light off the crystals on the chandelier. The small leaf motif from the silk window treatment is echoed on the walls with hand stenciling.
Photograph by Geoffrey Hodgdon

Aniko **Gaal Schott**

A.GAAL & ASSOCIATES

If ever there was a virtuoso in the realm of design, certainly Aniko Gaal Schott is that woman. An artist turned interior designer; her paintings have been exhibited and collected both nationally and internationally, as well as represented in the collection of The National Museum of Women in the Arts.

Aniko's career progressed from painter to the world of fashion as Vice President of the once famed Grafinckel's Stores, then to interior design. Her artistic eye, refined taste, sense of style, many years of international travel and the exposure to the most beautiful homes in the world, have crystallized into the force that is the power and the attraction behind her interior design business. In Washington where diplomacy is an industry, she has found her niche in designing interiors for embassy residences, having worked on some 10 embassies in the last 16 years. Presently she is in the processes of completing the spectacular 45,000-square-foot residence of The Embassy of The Republic of Turkey, "one of the most beautiful residences in Washington. "The home is a mansion filled with exquisite 16th-century paintings, 18th-century Tapestries, 19th-century wrought bronze work, elaborate carvings and collections of Sevres porcelain, Capo di Monte Urns and antique rugs. "A feast for the eye," said the acclaimed designer. "This three-year project has presented numerous challenges rarely seen in other design projects."

Her versatility in design varies from these projects to public buildings, sports arenas and work for a host of private clients. She and her associate, Elizabeth Balish, display a unique ability to bring spontaneity out of old, recognized pieces by applying the conventional in unconventional ways. A subtle yet enrapturing mix of antiques and contemporary pieces, infused with exquisite art creates interiors so delicious, they are almost savored on the palette as much as they are relished by the eye.

ABOVE:
The club-floor hallway (partial view) of The Verizon Center, Washington, D.C.
Photograph by Russell Hirshon

FACING PAGE:
Sitting room of the Residence of The Ambassador of The Netherlands.
Photograph by Gordon Beall

A. GAAL & ASSOCIATES
Aniko Gaal Schott
4803 Foxhall Crescent Court Northwest
Washington, D.C. 20007
202.333.3775
f: 202.333.2998

Claire Schwab

CLAIRE SCHWAB INTERIOR DESIGN

Claire Schwab's exposure to design began while growing up in Charlotte, North Carolina where her parents' home was decorated with several pieces from the shop of her grandfather, an Atlanta-based furniture maker and antiques dealer. After graduating from Vanderbilt with a degree in communications, Claire worked in the home furnishings division of Laura Ashley in London. There, reviewing furnishings before customer delivery, she learned firsthand how to recognize the hallmarks of quality and craftsmanship.

After a move to Washington, D.C., she found her London experience dovetailing with her lifelong love of sewing and fabric. While working as the communications director for a trade association, she began working through the Washington, D.C. Laura Ashley store, sewing soft furnishings such as duvets and dust ruffles and slowly amassing a following. She soon left her full-time job to focus on her business and obtain a degree in interior design.

LEFT:
Newly designed addition in McLean, Virginia just minutes from the CIA headquarters. Two prestigious lawyers expanded their home so the wife could have her own retreat! The bare windows showcase the architecture and the well-appointed hardscape and garden. Bright, cheerful fabrics and comfortable upholstery provide the relaxed feel she desired.

Claire discovered her background in fabrication and work as a seamstress informed her abilities to accurately appraise the scale and proportions of a space to show the room to its best advantage. Additionally, her deep understanding of the inner workings of window treatments gave her increased ease in working with workrooms and installers.

She opened Old Town Window Treatments in Alexandria, a name calculated to establish a comfort level with prospective clients. Claire realized that once people saw her expertise with window treatments, the costliest component of an interior, and enjoyed her level of service they would opt to have her do more. The shop also provided the perfect environment to meet clients and share her aesthetic in a welcoming environment.

Claire continues this approach, now working from her state-of-the art studio located on the lower level of her Alexandria Georgian home. Designed and built to her specifications, her fully decorated home is her working portfolio where clients can experience different seating styles and see a plethora of fabrics. In the 2,000-square-foot studio, clients can review fabric books and catalogs, including those from North Carolina manufacturers that help keep prices competitive.

Claire describes her approach as traditional with customized flair. With her eye and training she creates pleasing illusions that enhance existing spaces. A raised valance, for example, can make a ceiling seem taller; custom details like trimming and banding can provide the unexpected accent that enlivens a room.

TOP RIGHT:
Morning room for a recently remodeled home in Alexandria, Virginia. All is from Hickory Chair with Greeff fabric. The sun hits this room at just the perfect time.
Photograph courtesy of Claire Schwab Interior Design

BOTTOM RIGHT:
The soft yellow and tan hues in this living room provide warmth on the north-facing side of the house. Inherited furniture was reupholstered and trimmed. Silk drapes and woven shades soften the windows and also provide a more comfortable and relaxed feel. Sisal rug with tapestry border outlines and lightens the space.
Photograph courtesy of Claire Schwab Interior Design

FACING PAGE LEFT:
Sponsored by the Women's Committee for the National Symphony Orchestra, this showhouse resided in Potomac, Maryland. The lady's master bath project entailed removing a low, outdated vanity with mirror and lights, replacing it with lighter, higher ones, and improving the paint, lighting, and window coverings.
Photograph courtesy of Claire Schwab Interior Design

FACING PAGE RIGHT:
The designer and her husband designed and built this Georgian house in 2000. The mouldings, open two-story feel, and curved staircase reflect their classic taste. The bannisters, stained black, carry through the black accents throughout the house. Ellipses and ornate moulding highlight the doorways.
Photograph courtesy of Claire Schwab Interior Design

Claire's interiors possess a comfortable lived-in look. She is drawn to accessories that look collected and not new, and she works with those things clients treasure and have on hand. One of her personal most-prized accessories is a Tiffany bowl, recieved as a wedding gift filled with coral shells from her honeymoon. She is a believer in putting out family photographs—sometimes reframing them to provide pleasing updates—and pieces of one's personal history to provide the window into clients' lives that give each home its unique warmth. Needlepoint pillows, monogrammed towels and sheets and antiques add a sense of history, continuity.

Claire's firm is young: she and her two designers at 40, 31 and 30, respectively, possess an energy, excitement and openness that shines through in their work. Always learning, they immerse themselves in design challenges and remain open to

innovation. For example, they have recently been researching advances in plasma and infra-red for a number of media room projects they are at work on.

From childhood on, Claire's ophthalmologist father encouraged her to find a job she truly loved, telling her if she did she would never work a day in her life. Claire notes that his advice shaped her life. "The day everything is installed and the client hugs you and tells you they're happy, you can't beat that. That's as good as it gets."

Q&A
More about Claire ...

WHAT IS THE GREATEST PROFESSIONAL COMPLIMENT YOU HAVE RECEIVED?
Whether it is a showhouse room, tabletop display or an arrangement in my own home, I constantly enjoy hearing how lived in and personal my designs feel.

WHAT COLOR BEST DESCRIBES YOU?
Pomegranate red. It is rich and warm and infused with energy and fullness of life. This shade makes everything around it look rich and warm, too. I feel it perfectly sums my personality up.

WHAT BOOK ARE YOU READING NOW?
Other than baby books for my new infant, I am rereading *The Chronicles of Narnia*, by C.S. Lewis. I loved them as a child and have decorated the nursery for my new son in Brunschwig & Fils' "Narnia" fabric.

WHAT IS THE SINGLE THING YOU WOULD DO TO BRING A DULL HOUSE TO LIFE?
Update and install new window treatments (fabric or woven shades). They provide a custom look, updated decoration, and enliven a dull setting or calm an untamed one.

CLAIRE SCHWAB INTERIOR DESIGN
Claire Schwab, ASID, IDS
9059 Tower House Place
Alexandria, MD 22308
703.780.8767
www.claireschwab.com

ABOVE:
Family heirlooms feature silhouettes and bronzed shoes.

FACING PAGE:
The hand-painted red strie walls accentuate the appetite and stimulate good conversation in this dining room. Custom-made round table from Harden Furniture seats up to eight and is distressed to look like an English antique. Chairs and servers are from Hickory Chair. Antique hunt rug brings in colors found throughout the first floor. Silk draperies and valances accentuate the tall ceilings and elegantly frame the windows.

Gwen **Seidlitz**

SAGE

"The name Sage has nothing to do with the herb or color," says Gwen Seidlitz, owner of Sage in Great Falls, Virginia, as she relays the story of her business. The "concept" of opening a store/showroom/boutique happened amazingly enough, seven years ago. The name Sage was an inspiration to her when, in the spring of 2000, an antique dealer strongly encouraged Gwen to share her vision with the community. When a store front soon appeared in her ideal location, Gwen was able to make a decision about her career in a very short amount of time.

Gwen's definition of Sage is intuitive wisdom, both from herself and extracted from her clients. Her primary design goal is to create living spaces that make a house a home. She accomplishes this while creating comfort, luxury and detail in a family's everyday space that is practical and beautiful. Believing that you should not have to forsake comfort for beauty, Gwen strives to enhance functionality in all aspects of the home. She believes a home is not only for, but all about the family and in each project moves away from the untouchable rooms of yesteryear.

A work of art in itself, the Sage showroom serves as a natural reflection of Gwen's design capabilities and flair for the comfortable, yet elegant. Many clients visit Sage for its reputation of offering unique furniture and accessories and are then pleased to discover that Gwen also offers home design consults. Starting with priorities, Gwen visits the home and assesses where the individual or family will be spending the most time. Using this as her starting point, she begins the design process and chooses furniture and accessories according to the client's preferences and lifestyle.

ABOVE:
A close-up shot of this Dino Mark Anthony chair highlights the Brazilian side table and other fine, yet important design elements.
Photograph by Mark Finkenstadt

FACING PAGE:
This luxurious family room is centered around the cozy stone fireplace. Dino Mark Anthony leather and chenille sectional, Woodland coffee table and fine arts lamp and chandelier complete the detail of the room.
Photograph by Mark Finkenstadt

Gwen also offers a service unique to Sage: Accessory Runs. After visiting and photographing the house, she or one of her highly qualified staff will return to her showroom, choose the accessories and return to the home, placing all of the new accents in just the right place to suit the environment. The accessories from the showroom are often just what a client is looking for to complete their interiors. When Gwen sees the "WOW" look on her clients' faces, she knows she has done her job.

Despite the upscale offerings at Gwen's showroom, she likes to keep the atmosphere relaxed. Her husband has even referred to her style as "Gwen Shui," playing on the term feng shui, the Chinese art of placement. "We have a relaxed atmosphere and we get to know each client, establishing a personal relationship by listening to their needs and understanding their lifestyle," the designer explained. While Sage Interiors offers dining room tables and gigantic armoires in excess of $20,000, Gwen also stocks the store with accent pieces for any budget. From a $9 desktop photograph holder to a $46 set of marble coasters to an iron candelabra complete with flower detailing and crystal accents for $250, Gwen caters to the amount any customer will feel comfortable spending.

As a testament to Gwen's innate eye for design, she, along with a select few other designers, was invited to participate in the National Symphony Orchestra Decorators' Showhouse for three consecutive years from 2003 to 2005. The invitation to design a room in the showhouse is extended only to the area's best designers. Gwen's design of the 2005 house's media room was so exquisite it was featured in *The Washington Post*. Despite the 110-inch Vutec screen and Dolby Digital/DTS Surround System, the focus of the room was obviously Gwen's dramatic design of velvet mohair walls in a tasteful shade of chartreuse accompanied by faux fur throws on chenille club chairs.

ABOVE LEFT:
This sunroom invites intimate, quiet reflection. The serene color scheme creates the mood complemented by the Fine Arts lamp, JM Paquet sofa and Provence coffee table.
Photograph by Mark Finkenstadt

ABOVE RIGHT:
This dining room, perfect for casual or formal dining, boasts a Provence dining table and Woodland dining chairs.
Photograph by Mark Finkenstadt

FACING PAGE:
These Dino Mark Anthony chairs and ottomans combine a unique blend of pattern, texture and color, adding warmth to any space, and most especially for this family room.
Photograph by Mark Finkenstadt

In addition to *The Washington Post*, Gwen's stellar work has also been published in *Elan, Connection* and *Home & Design*. Gwen is not only known for her quality work; her reputation as a customer friendly, easily approachable designer often precedes her. Her ability to make profound connections with her clients keeps them returning to Sage again and again. Going the extra mile to make her clients happy is second nature to Gwen; in fact, it is her design philosophy that "the perfect mix of luxury and comfort are just a result of effortless, wise advice."

ABOVE LEFT:
This handsome bar cleverly marries the kitchen and family rooms architecturally.
Photograph by Mark Finkenstadt

ABOVE RIGHT:
A lovely vantage point of this master suite highlights the beautiful coral red/black contrast of the clean, understated Dino Mark Anthony chairs, ottomans and bench. Luxurious fabrics and a Fine Arts lamp lend the perfect blend of intimacy and serenity that should be present in every master suite.
Photograph by Mark Finkenstadt

FACING PAGE:
This media room was designed to offer the versatility of its intended purpose or to double as a club-like floor plan for entertaining. Luxurious Highland Court velvet mohair walls are angled with cuts to enhance the shape of the Fine Arts wall sconces. Dino Mark Anthony chairs, ottomans and bench.
Photograph by Mark Finkenstadt

Q&A

More about Gwen ...

WHAT PERSONAL INDULGENCE DO YOU SPEND THE MOST MONEY ON?
Books and cashmere.

NAME ONE THING MOST PEOPLE DON'T KNOW ABOUT YOU.
I have a serious addiction to jelly beans!

YOU WOULDN'T KNOW IT, BUT MY FRIENDS WOULD TELL YOU I ...
Like my down time.

WHAT PHILOSOPHY HAVE YOU STUCK WITH FOR YEARS THAT STILL WORKS FOR YOU TODAY?
If you love it, you can make it work!

SAGE
Gwen Seidlitz
10135 Calvin Run Road
Great Falls, VA 22066
703.757.0558
f: 703.757.0449
www.sageinteriors.com

Dee Thornton
HOUSEWORKS INTERIORS

First trained as an educator, Dee Thornton, founder and principal of Houseworks Interiors, now identifies her background and interest in English literature as an early attempt to satisfy the aesthetic impulses that guide and define her passion for interior design. In 1989, she completed her degree in interior design at Mount Vernon College, now George Washington University. There she first discovered a special interest in lighting principles which she further honed in her work with architectural lighting consultants. "I always think about what lighting will best serve the functionality of a room; from general ambient lighting to the details of task lighting and special accent lighting."

The cornerstone of Dee's design philosophy is developing an understanding of the client's lifestyle while respecting the architectural envelope. Her client-sensitive designs put the client's needs and desires in the context of the house in a beautiful, livable way. In creating furniture plans that value the scale of the home, she first looks at how people move through their space, observing their particular rules of passage—and plans accordingly.

Ensuring that each room is as beautiful—and livable—as possible, Dee also makes certain that each client is able to bring their personal style to the process. Using

pieces her clients currently own and treasure along with fabrics and patterns that evoke fond memories, her clients' style is central to the home's design. By listening carefully to their thoughts and ideas, Dee helps her clients "achieve a look that transcends the commonplace and surpasses the chic." The end result of this process is a home which reflects the individuality of her clients, as well as Dee's artistic flair and years of experience.

ABOVE:
Mingling old and new, the aged finish of an Italian chandelier contrasts with polished mahogany and host/hostess chairs upholstered in an abstract floral woven fabric.
Photograph by Gwin Hunt

FACING PAGE:
Tonal lilac walls enlivened with chocolate, pumpkin and spice sets the mood for this living room. Clean-lined upholstery relaxes the more formal wood furnishings, while a Venetian glass bowl adds sparkle.
Photograph by Gwin Hunt

While Dee is comfortable working in a range of styles, most of what she does is forward looking, new traditional; a mixture venturing beyond eclectic, expressing traditional forms in unexpected fabrics, textures and surfaces. Complementary textures such as chenilles, velvets, wools, silks and linens take on a stronger role, combining to key off one another, highlight the furniture forms and direct the eye around the room. The overall look of the space is clean, but layered and complex.

ABOVE:
Renovation of this Watergate, Washington, D.C. residence converted a large closet to a library niche for the owner's custom yew wood baby grand piano. Neutral walls and textured, sculptural upholstery serve to expand the space and highlight the art and Tibetan rugs.
Photograph by Gwin Hunt

FACING PAGE TOP:
The Potomac River is viewed across a round dining table which was custom made to complement a rare set of antique Biedermeier chairs. A contemporary gilded chandelier provides counterpoint.
Photograph by Gwin Hunt

FACING PAGE BOTTOM:
The fully renovated galley-style kitchen features custom cherry cabinetry, sleek glass tile and granite counters. Brazilian hardwood cherry floors were set on an angle to visually broaden the space, while curvilinear track lighting adds movement and drama.
Photograph by Gwin Hunt

Q&A

More about Dee ...

WHAT IS THE MOST UNUSUAL DESIGN OR TECHNIQUE YOU'VE USED IN ONE OF YOUR PROJECTS?
I often engage unique tile designs for bathrooms. We do our best to thoroughly plan before embarking on a project, but eyes-on and hands-on in the field during installation is critical to a successful design.

WHAT IS THE SINGLE THING YOU WOULD DO TO BRING A DULL HOUSE TO LIFE?
Paint! It is, without a doubt, the most cost-effective, high-impact design tool.

WHAT DO YOU LIKE MOST ABOUT DOING BUSINESS IN YOUR LOCALE?
The metropolitan Washington, D.C. area has sophisticated consumers with varied tastes from all over the globe. It makes work and life very interesting and challenging.

WHAT IS THE HIGHEST COMPLIMENT YOU'VE RECEIVED PROFESSIONALLY?
It is always fulfilling to receive a thank you from a client for understanding their lifestyle and taste.

WHAT ONE ELEMENT OF STYLE HAVE YOU STUCK WITH FOR YEARS THAT STILL WORKS FOR YOU TODAY?
A constant in my career as a designer has been respecting the architectural design and proportions of the space being designed.

YOU WOULDN'T KNOW IT, BUT MY FRIENDS WOULD TELL YOU I AM ...
Definitely a perfectionist!

HOUSEWORKS INTERIORS
Dee Thornton
412 South Washington Street
Alexandria, VA 22314
703.519.1900
f: 703.519.3533
www.houseworksinteriors.com

Marlies **Venute**

MARLIES VENUTE INTERIORS, INC.

Marlies Venute, FIFDA, founder of Marlies Venute Interior Design, Inc., brings her internationally influenced design style to each project she designs throughout the Washington, D.C. area. Born and raised in Germany, Marlies established her firm in 1989 in McLean, Virginia after living abroad for 12 years. While living overseas with her husband Don, daughter Jeannine and son Stephen in La Paz, Bolivia, Asuncion, Paraguay and Bonn, Germany, she practiced interior design and established her international portfolio with clients such as the Bank of America in Paraguay, Shell Oil and the Ambassador's Residence in Bonn, Germany, as well as numerous private clients.

With a faithful client base which spans across 20 years, Marlies' design philosophies are well respected among both her clients and colleagues. Featured in publications such as *Metropolitan Home, Traditional Homes, Home & Design Magazine, The Washington Post* and *Columbus Times*, Marlies' hallmark style of contemporary furniture and modern classics mixed with ethnic artifacts and good lighting easily makes her clients' homes into dream homes.

"Good interior design should reveal an individual's identity, not erase it. My primary goal is to ensure the substance of my client's life is incorporated in each project.

Whether you are seeking small refinements to your present decor or a complete redesign, you should be confident that everything will reflect and interpret your own personal tastes and lifestyle," said the well-known designer.

Working closely with her clients, Marlies couples teamwork and creative design to generate a beautiful new product. While Marlies and her team handle the most complex design and remodeling needs, she keeps her firm small enough to deliver truly personalized service.

ABOVE:
A mix of old and new in a spectacular townhouse at the edge of Georgetown in Washington, D.C.
Photograph by John Smith

FACING PAGE:
The 1999 Alexandria Showhouse features an Ingo Maurer light made of rice paper and chairs by Palazetti, Inc.
Photograph by Gordon Beall

Q&A

More about Marlies ...

WHAT DO YOU LIKE MOST ABOUT DOING BUSINESS IN YOUR LOCALE?
The international and ethnically diverse community of the greater Washington area is exhilarating.

YOU WOULDN'T KNOW IT, BUT MY FRIENDS WOULD TELL YOU I AM ...
Taller in person.

NAME ONE THING MOST PEOPLE DON'T KNOW ABOUT YOU.
I have two beautiful granddaughters who live in Thailand and keep me traveling.

WHAT COLOR BEST DESCRIBES YOU AND WHY?
Sky blue; it goes with anything. There are no limitations and it encompasses everything.

WHAT IS A SINGLE THING YOU WOULD DO TO BRING A DULL HOUSE TO LIFE?
Give it light!

Photograph by John Smith

MARLIES VENUTE INTERIORS, INC.
Marlies Venute, FIFDA
6819 Elm Street, Suite 6
McLean, VA 22101
703.821.2427
www.venuteinteriors.com

Before moving to the United States from Germany, Marlies graduated from the Cologne Institute of Design. She has since become a longstanding member of the International Furnishings and Design Association, Washington, D.C. Chapter and in 2004, was elected Chapter President. As a testament to her dedication to the community, Marlies is also a member of the Virginia office of Partnerships, where she helps to bridge the digital divide in low cost housing areas by designing and implementing learning centers with other industry partners.

Since arriving in Washington in 1988, Marlies has left her mark on many prominent spaces in the area, including the Chateauville Foundation in Casselton, Virginia designed for Maestro Lorin Maazel, the AOL headquarters (lobbies, signage and executive offices) and the Washington Speakers Bureau in Alexandria, Virginia. Marlies' work has also taken her beyond the greater Washington, D.C. area, across the United States and the Eastern Shore, like Rehoboth and Bethany Beach in Delaware.

ABOVE:
Corner of a living room in Great Falls, Virginia. Contemporary chairs by Giorgetti surround a hydraulic table that adjusts for the need of the occasion. A sculptural vessel by Berman floats on a slice of acrylic on a pedestal.
Photograph by John Smith

FACING PAGE:
Lobby of AOL Headquarters in Sterling, Virginia after the total redesign from "Classic Corporate" before to the "Internet Generation" of today.
Photograph by Omar Salinas

Margery **Wedderburn**

MARGERY WEDDERBURN INTERIORS

A Washingtonian since 1986, Margery Wedderburn began her career working for a Senator on Capitol Hill. She soon realized that despite her interest in politics and her focus on international business, her passion was to be involved in a more creative field.

The daughter of an American decorative arts collector and lecturer, Margery has grown up absorbing by osmosis the fine points of furnishings and design, making the subsequent shift to interior design a natural one. During her graduate school work at Mount Vernon, now part of George Washington University, she studied and worked with some of the area's foremost designers, including Mary Douglas Drysdale and Thomas Pheasant, before becoming part of Marriott International's Architecture & Construction team.

Based on this solid foundation, Margery launched her own company in 1999, focusing on creating transitional interiors with a balanced mix of contemporary and traditional influences. An innovative use of color, space and transitional furniture, such as that designed by Niermann Weeks, with their subtle reinterpretation of enduring design provides the kind of focal point Margery likes to make central to her projects.

"When we enter our homes, " Margery states, "there should be an immediate emotional connection to the space. In the early phase of a project I will work with my clients to help them think through what that connection might be, and it is different for almost every client. For some it is a feeling of vibrancy or strength. Others want a sense of space. For many people, especially in the greater D.C. area, it is a more subtle feeling of relaxation, a release from the stress that engulfs contemporary life." That stress can be replaced by a sense of style and a reconnection that comes from being in a space that reflects the client's true self.

Balance, harmony and comfort: these guiding themes are evident throughout Margery's work. Their careful blending with the clients' personal vision makes every design unique. Livability is key to Margery. She brings the outdoors in by capturing

ABOVE:
Tea room, Washington Design Center Showhouse. Baker chair and floor lamp. Two five-legged Asian tables bring good luck, Randolph & Hein, through Holly Hunt showroom.
Photograph by Lydia Cutter

FACING PAGE:
Sunroom in a Potomac, Maryland home. The Flensted mobile adds quiet motion to the room, through Nielsen Trading. Nesting tables and floor lamp, Niermann Weeks. Italian chaise, DAR International. Flowers from Petal Works of Great Falls, Virginia.
Photograph by Gwin Hunt

ABOVE:
Margery's home in Virginia. A harpist since her childhood, Margery displays her harp as an art object here. Tea table created and constructed by Margery's father. Original Australian Aboriginal artwork.
Photograph by Gwin Hunt

FACING PAGE:
Sunroom in Potomac, Maryland. Sea glass art framed photographs by Celia Pearson, through Jayson Fifteen Showroom, Washington Design Center. Art accessories through Niermann Weeks. Celadon bowl through Baker.
Photograph by Gwin Hunt

Q&A

More about Margery ...

WHAT PERSONAL INDULGENCE DO YOU SPEND THE MOST MONEY ON?

Never ask someone who is a mother of young children AND who runs a design business this question. Two hours to myself is a personal indulgence. When I find the time, I treat myself to personal training sessions or some beautiful clothes.

NAME ONE THING MOST PEOPLE DON'T KNOW ABOUT YOU.

Maintaining a high level of fitness helps me keep my energy level up throughout the day. Most people don't now I have a secret double life as an aerobics instructor—I have been teaching for about 14 years and even worked as a personal trainer during graduate school. My husband and I used to joke that when I started my own interior design company it should be an interior design and personal training firm and the slogan should be, 'Have a good-looking home and look good in it.'

WHAT COLOR BEST DESCRIBES YOU?

It would have to be a painting, actually. Yellow for its fresh exuberance, and eggshell blue for its calm, atmospheric quality. The two colors together strike a nice balance; very yin and yang.

YOU CAN TELL I LIVE IN WASHINGTON, D.C. BECAUSE ...

I love good, classical design presented in a fresh, new way, love meeting people from all over the world and, of course, love to dive into a good political debate.

WHAT ARE YOU READING NOW?

The *Harry Potter* series (with my boys); *The Time Traveler's Wife*, by Audrey Niffenegger and *Objects of Design* from the Museum of Modern Art.

MARGERY WEDDERBURN INTERIORS, LLC
Margery Wedderburn, ASID
Vienna, VA 22182
703.757.5001
f: 703.757.5801
www.margerywedderburninteriors.com

nature in such elements as bamboo floors, fabrics in an earth palette or a print inspired by nature. Light also plays into her designs—allowing light, for example, to filter through an arrangement of glass pieces. She also likes to incorporate images of water—the ocean, a pool, a lake; this strategic use of artwork can also enhance the connection between indoors and out.

Margery's work has been featured in such magazines and showhouses as *Home and Design, Home and Design Guidebooks*, 2005 and 2006, and the 2003 Fall Design House, Washington Design Center. Her work is also featured in *Decorator Show Houses*, by Tina Skinner, Melissa Cardona and Nancy Ottino.

"My focus is on the client's vision and discovering the type of environment they are looking to create in their homes," says Margery. "What do they want their spaces to say, to make them feel when they enter? Helping clients find that in their lives is what gets me excited about this business."

publishing team

Brian G. Carabet, Publisher
John A. Shand, Publisher
Phil Reavis, Executive Publisher
Kathryn Newell, Senior Associate Publisher

Michele Cunningham-Scott, Art Director
Mary Elizabeth Acree, Graphic Designer
Emily Kattan, Graphic Designer
Benito Quintanilla, Graphic Designer

Elizabeth Gionta, Managing Editor
Rosalie Wilson, Editor
Lauren Castelli, Editor
Anita Kasmar, Editor

Kristy Randall, Senior Production Coordinator
Laura Greenwood, Production Coordinator
Jennifer Lenhart, Production Coordinator
Jessica Garrison, Traffic Coordinator

Carol Kendall, Project Manager
Beverly Smith, Project Manager

PANACHE PARTNERS, LLC
CORPORATE OFFICE
13747 Montfort Drive
Suite 100
Dallas, TX 75240
972.661.9884
www.panache.com

WASHINGTON OFFICE
856.316.6069

DESIGNER: José Solis, Solis Betancourt, *Page 83*

The PANACHE Portfolio

The catalog of fine books in the areas of interior design and architecture and design continues to grow for Panache Partners, LLC. With more than 30 books published or in production, look for one or more of these keepsake books in a market near you.

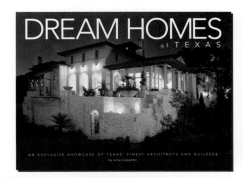

Spectacular Homes Series

Published in 2005
Spectacular Homes of Georgia
Spectacular Homes of South Florida
Spectacular Homes of Tennessee
Spectacular Homes of Texas

Published or Publishing in 2006
Spectacular Homes of California
Spectacular Homes of the Carolinas
Spectacular Homes of Chicago
Spectacular Homes of Colorado
Spectacular Homes of Florida
Spectacular Homes of Michigan
Spectacular Homes of the Pacific Northwest
Spectacular Homes of Greater Philadelphia
Spectacular Homes of the Southwest

Other titles available from Panache Partners

Spectacular Hotels
Texans and Their Pets
Spectacular Restaurants of Texas

Dream Homes Series

Published in 2005
Dream Homes of Texas

Published or Publishing in 2006
Dream Homes of Colorado
Dream Homes of South Florida
Dream Homes New Jersey
Dream Homes New York
Dream Homes Greater Philadelphia
Dream Homes Western Deserts

Order two or more copies today and we'll pay the shipping.

To order visit www.panache.com
or call 972.661.9884.

PANACHE
PANACHE PARTNERS, LLC
Creating Spectacular Publications for Discerning Readers

index of designers

DESIGNER: Lisa Bartolomei, Bartolomei and Company, *Page 17*